D0792442

PROBLEM
SOLVING
in
MATHEMATICS

Cover design by Bev and Charles Dana

This work was developed under an ESEA Title IVC grant from the Oregon Department of Education, Office of Policy and Program Development. The content, however, does not necessarily reflect the position or policy of the Oregon Department of Education and no official endorsement of these materials should be inferred.

Distribution for this work was arranged by LINC Resources, Inc.

ISBN 0-86651-187-3

Order Number DS01413

5 6 7 8 9 10 11 12 13 14-MA-95 94 93 92 91

DALE
SEYMOUR
PUBLICATIONS
P.O. BOX 10888
PALO ALTO, CA 94303

PROBLEM SOLVING IN MATHEMATICS

PROJECT STAFF

DIRECTOR: OSCAR SCHAAF, UNIVERSITY OF OREGON
ASSOCIATE DIRECTOR: RICHARD BRANNAN, LANE EDUCATION SERVICE DISTRICT

WRITERS: RICHARD BRANNAN
                      MARYANN DEBRICK
                      JUDITH JOHNSON
                      GLENDA KIMERLING
                      SCOTT McFADDEN
                      JILL McKENNEY
                      OSCAR SCHAAF
                      MARY ANN TODD

PRODUCTION: MEREDITH SCHAAF
                      BARBARA STOEFFLER

EVALUATION: HENRY DIZNEY
                      ARTHUR MITTMAN
                      JAMES ELLIOTT
                      LESLIE MAYES
                      ALISTAIR PEACOCK

PROJECT GRADUATE   FRANK DEBRICK
    STUDENTS: MAX GILLETT
                      KEN JENSEN
                      PATTY KINCAID
                      CARTER McCONNELL
                      TOM STONE

ACKNOWLEDGMENTS:

TITLE IV-C LIAISON: Ray Talbert
                         Charles Nelson

                         Monitoring Team

                         Charles Barker
                         Ron Clawson
                         Jeri Dickerson
                         Anthony Fernandez
                         Richard Olson
                         Ralph Parrish
                         Fred Rugh
                         Alton Smedstad

ADVISORY COMMITTEE: Mary Grace Kantowski   University of Florida
                         John LeBlanc   Indiana University
                         Richard Lesh   Northwestern University
                         Edwin McClintock   Florida International University
                         Len Pikaart   Ohio University
                         Kenneth Vos   The College of St. Catherine

A special thanks is due to the many teachers, schools, and districts within
the state of Oregon that have participated in the development and evaluation
of the project materials. A list would be lengthy and certainly someone's
name would inadvertently be omitted. Those persons involved have the project's
heartfelt thanks for an impossible job well done.

The following projects and/or persons are thanked for their willingness to
share pupil materials, evaluation materials, and other ideas.

    Don Fineran, Mathematics Consultant, Oregon Department of Education
    Frank Lester, Indiana University
    Steve Meiring, Mathematics Consultant, Ohio Department of Education
    Harold Schoen, University of Iowa
    Iowa Problem Solving Project, Earl Ockenga, Manager
    Math Lab Curriculum for Junior High, Dan Dolan, Director
    Mathematical Problem Solving Project, John LeBlanc, Director

CONTENTS

CONTENTS

INTRODUCTION

The activities in this book are designed for the low-achieving math pupil. Many are similar to activities in the regular books except the math computation and length of time needed for completion are scaled down. You will find six sections: Drill and Practice (with whole numbers) Story Problems; Tangrams; Patterns; Geometry; and Challenge Problems. The Drill and Practice and the Geometry sections can be used in any order you choose. The activities in the other sections are best used in the order they occur and by using all the activities in the section.

The demand for these materials came from teachers using the regular PSM materials. They said their low achievers really liked doing problem-solving activities. They also said their low achievers were able to learn and use problem-solving skills, even for solving challenge problems. But more materials at a level more appropriate to the low achiever's math skills were needed; thus this book. You will find no grade-level suggestions for the activities. Field test comments from teachers in grades 4-6 indicated the activities were appropriate for all three grades. In fact, several third-grade teachers have successfully used the materials as well as many teachers of average and above pupils in grades 4-6.

Use of these materials follows the instructional approach advocated for all the materials developed by the PSM staff. First, teach specific problem-solving skills such as guess and check, look for a pattern, etc. The lessons for this instruction are found in the regular PSM books. Second, practice those skills with activities integrated with the basic skills being taught. Third, apply those skills in the solution of challenge problems. Many of the lessons in the book can be used for this third purpose.

Teachers do find the instruction needed with low achievers on problem-solving activities more direct than that used with regular or gifted pupils. Often, working the first couple of problems with the class is necessary. Certainly a teacher needs to be ready to offer helpful hints or guiding questions. Also, many of the activities call for a manipulative such as tangrams, cut-out shapes, movable number disks, etc. All these allow the low achiever to search for and find the correct solution before any recording of results is done.

A final comment is needed. These materials are not a substitute for the activities in the regular books. Indeed, teachers have found low achievers able to do many of those lessons. These materials simply provide you with a resource of more materials to use. Repeated experience and successful completion seem to be two keys to developing pupils who are good problem solvers.

I. DRILL AND PRACTICE

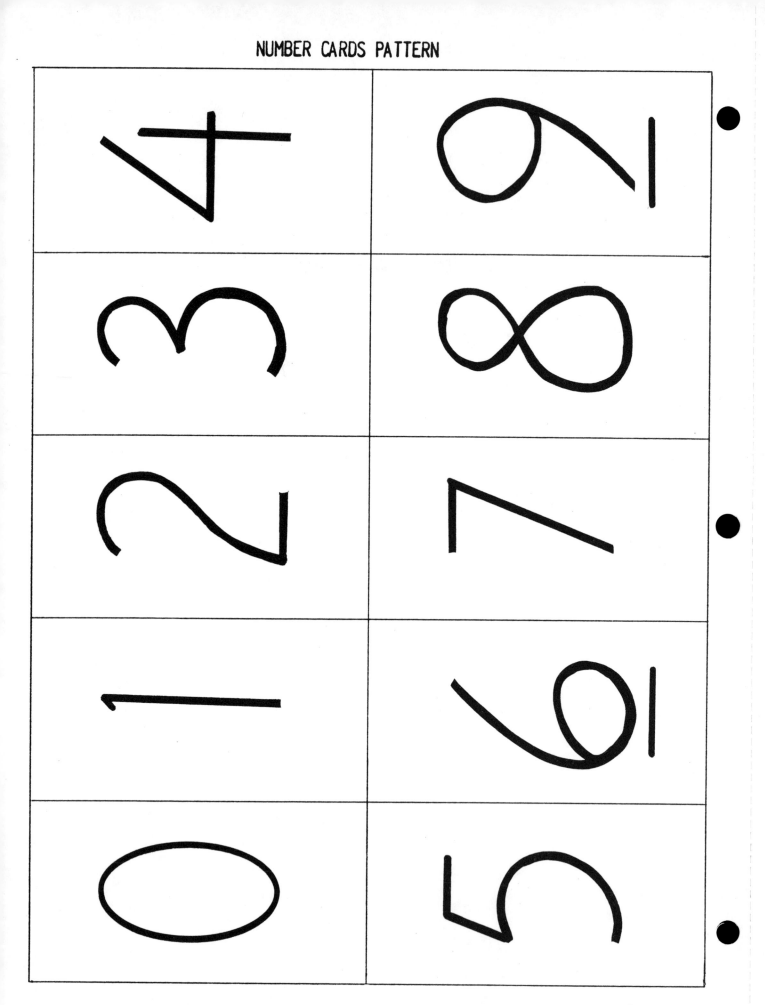

© PSM 81

NUMBER HUNT

```
  12        19        6        11
                  5
            4              18
  17            21
        13              7        20
```

Find two numbers on the sign whose

1. sum is 24 _____ _____

2. sum is 20 _____ _____

3. sum is 7 less than 25 _____ _____

4. sum is 8 more than 17 _____ _____

5. difference is 11 _____ _____

6. difference is 14 _____ _____

7. difference is 2 more than 8 _____ _____

8. difference is 2 less than 11 _____ _____

9. sum is 22 and difference is 14 _____ _____

10. sum is 25 and difference is 13 _____ _____

11. sum is 16 and difference is 6 _____ _____

EXTENSION   Use the back of this page.
             Make a new number sign.
             Write some "number hunt" questions to go with the sign.

Number Hunt

Mathematics teaching objectives:

. Use place value concepts to make reasonable estimates.

. Use mathematics vocabulary (sum and difference).

Problem-solving skills pupils might use:

. Guess and check.

. Make reasonable estimates.

Materials needed:

. None

Comments and suggestions:

. Work a few problems together as a class and then have pupils finish the page on their own or by working with a partner.

. Some pupils may need encouragement to continue to "guess and check" until they find solutions to parts i, j, and k.

Answers:

a.	19	5
b.	13	7
c.	6	12
d.	5	20
e.	18	7
f.	4	18
g.	21	11
h.	20	11
i.	4	18
j.	19	6
k.	5	11

FIVE TOSSES

Your teacher will give you a special worksheet with workspace for four games.

Here are the directions for each game:

- Your teacher will toss an ordinary die five times.
- After each toss, place the digit which lands face up in one of the three possible columns.
- After five tosses, add to find your total.
- The winner is the player whose total is closest to 500 <u>without</u> going over.

Below are the results of a game played by Pat and Lee.

Who won the game? _____

	Pat		
	100's	10's	1's
Toss #1		4	0
Toss #2	3	0	0
Toss #3			6
Toss #4		5	0
Toss #5			5
TOTAL			

	Lee		
	100's	10's	1's
Toss #1	4	0	0
Toss #2		3	0
Toss #3			6
Toss #4		5	0
Toss #5			5
TOTAL			

Five Tosses

Mathematics teaching objectives:

. Practice addition skills.

. Develop some informal probability concepts.

. Compare and order numbers.

Problem-solving skills pupils _might_ use:

. Recognize limits and eliminate possibilities.

. Apply what you know about addition and place value.

. Make decisions based upon data.

Materials needed:

. One ordinary die

Comments and suggestions:

. This is a teacher-directed large-group activity. Duplicate the directions and examples on an overlay. Tell pupils the object of the game is to find winning game strategies. Play two games; discuss winning strategies. Play one more game and again discuss. Play additional games to "test" the strategies.

. Rather than duplicating the charts you may choose to direct pupils to prepare their own.

. Pupils will need the ability to add a column of numbers involving "carrying"

Answers:

Pat's score is 401.

Lee's score is 491.

Lee won the game.

Game answers depend on the roll of the die and the placement of the numbers by the pupils. You can expect a number of "tie" games as pupils become proficient in their placement of numbers.

FIVE TOSSES WORKSHEET

Game 1

	100's	10's	1's
Toss #1			
Toss #2			
Toss #3			
Toss #4			
Toss #5			
TOTAL			

Game 2

	100's	10's	1's
Toss #1			
Toss #2			
Toss #3			
Toss #4			
Toss #5			
TOTAL			

Game 3

	100's	10's	1's
Toss #1			
Toss #2			
Toss #3			
Toss #4			
Toss #5			
TOTAL			

Game 4

	100's	10's	1's
Toss #1			
Toss #2			
Toss #3			
Toss #4			
Toss #5			
TOTAL			

Game 5

	100's	10's	1's
Toss #1			
Toss #2			
Toss #3			
Toss #4			
Toss #5			
TOTAL			

Game 6

	100's	10's	1's
Toss #1			
Toss #2			
Toss #3			
Toss #4			
Toss #5			
TOTAL			

FIVE TO MAKE 205

1. Your teacher has 2 regular dice.

    Your teacher will toss those dice 5 times.

    Each time your teacher tosses the dice,

    . use the digits which land face up to make a 2-digit number.

    . record the number.

    After 5 tosses, total the five 2-digit numbers.

    Winner is the player whose total is closest to 205 <u>without</u> <u>going</u> <u>over</u>.

Toss 1	_____
Toss 2	_____
Toss 3	_____
Toss 4	_____
Toss 5	_____
TOTAL	_____

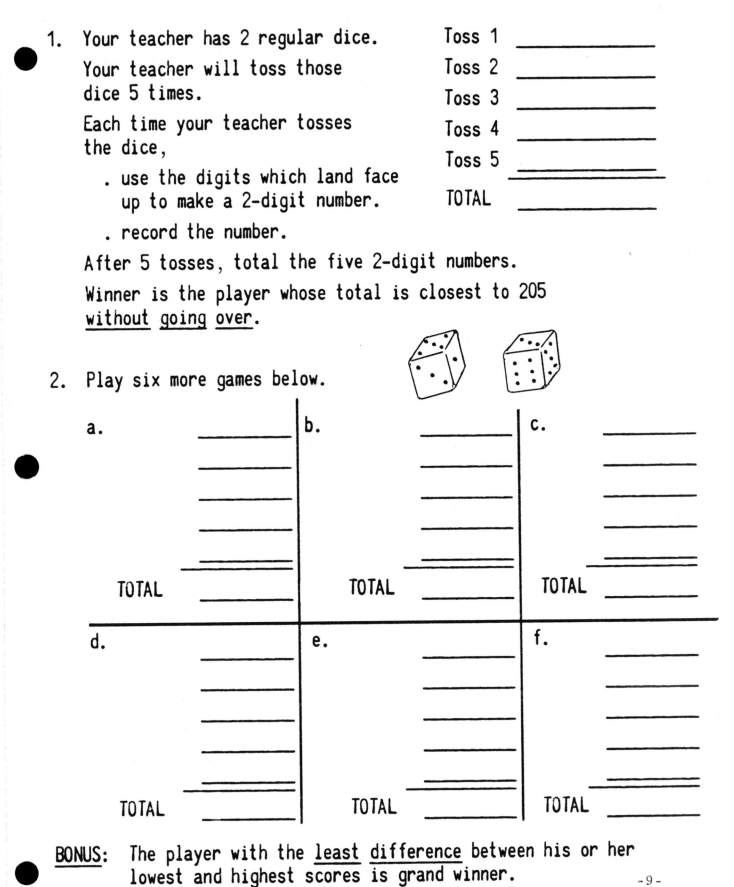

2. Play six more games below.

a. _____

_____

_____

_____

_____

TOTAL _____

b. _____

_____

_____

_____

_____

TOTAL _____

c. _____

_____

_____

_____

_____

TOTAL _____

d. _____

_____

_____

_____

_____

TOTAL _____

e. _____

_____

_____

_____

_____

TOTAL _____

f. _____

_____

_____

_____

_____

TOTAL _____

<u>BONUS</u>: The player with the <u>least</u> <u>difference</u> between his or her lowest and highest scores is grand winner.

-9-

Five To Make 205

Mathematics teaching objectives:

.Practice addition and subtraction skills.

.Develop some informal probability concepts (when to take a chance).

.Compare and order numbers.

Problem-solving skills pupils _might_ use:

.Recognize limits and eliminate possibilities.

.Apply what you know about place value and addition.

.Make reasonable estimates.

Materials needed:

.2 regular dice

Comments and suggestions:

.This is a whole-class activity.

.Prepare an overlay of the pupil page or duplicate for pupil use.

.Let the picture on the pupil page show the first toss. Ask "What different numbers could be recorded in the Toss 1 space?" Complete the introductory game taking suggestions from the class. The six games in part 2 are to be completed with each individual pupil making her/his own decisions.

.Pupils should be encouraged to find a winning game strategy.

Answers:

Answers will vary, depending on the roll of the dice.

"WORD" PROBLEMS

1. Use your calculator. Do this problem:

    Twenty-nine plus seven equals 3 __ .

2. Now do these:

    a. Sixteen plus thirty-two equals __ 8 .

    b. One hundred twenty-five plus eleven equals __ __ 6 .

    c. Three hundred four plus seventy-seven is __ 8 __ .

    d. Two hundred eighteen plus forty is __ __ 8 .

    e. Five hundred eighty plus sixteen plus four is 6 __ 0 .

    f. Six hundred twenty-five take away fourteen equals __ 1 1 .

    g. Five hundred fifty minus two hundred twelve is 3 __ 8 .

    h. Twenty-two subtracted from one hundred thirty-one is 1 __ 9 .

    i. Six hundred take away one hundred one is __ __ 9 .

    j. Sixty-seven plus three tens is 9 __ .

    k. Five tens plus six tens plus 25 ones is __ 3 __ .

    l. One hundred fifty-three take away one more than 49 is __ __ 3 .

    m. Seven hundred sixty-two plus ten more than 70 is 8 __ __ .

    n. Five hundred plus twenty less than sixty is 5 __ __ .

    o. Seven hundred sixteen plus twenty more than 90 is 8 __ __ .

EXTENSION

Use the back of the page. Write four "word" problems of
your own.
Solve the problems.
Write each answer —
. in numbers
. in words

"Word" Problems

Mathematics teaching objective:

. Use place value and expanded notation concepts.

Problem-solving skills pupils might use:

. Make decisions based upon data.

Materials:

. One calculator for each pair of pupils

Comments and suggestions:

. Work the first problems as a class. Have pupils finish the page working with a partner.

. When most pupils have completed the page, discuss solutions together and share any problems made up by pupils for the extension activity.

Answers:

1. 36

2. a. 48
    b. 136
    c. 381
    d. 258
    e. 600
    f. 611
    g. 338
    h. 109
    i. 499
    j. 97
    k. 135
    l. 103
    m. 842
    n. 540
    o. 826

PLACE THE DIGITS - A

Follow the directions your teacher gives.

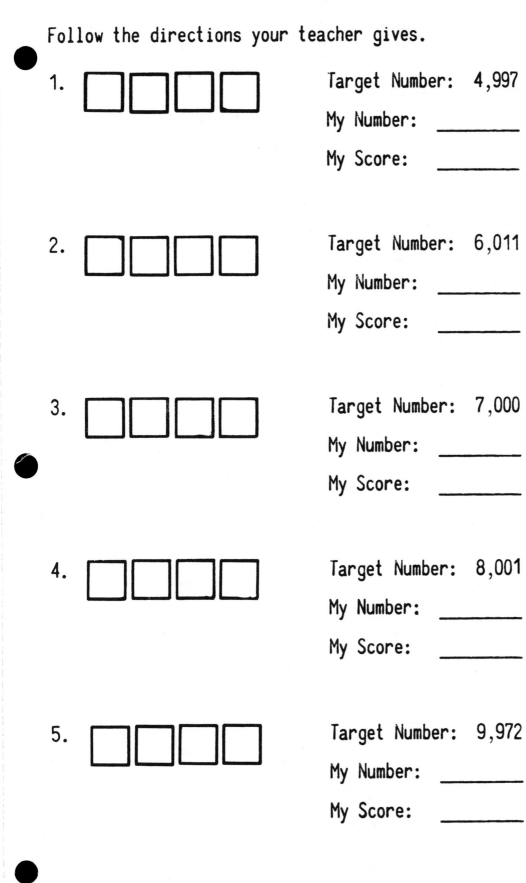

1. ☐☐☐☐

Target Number: 4,997

My Number: _____

My Score: _____

2. ☐☐☐☐

Target Number: 6,011

My Number: _____

My Score: _____

3. ☐☐☐☐

Target Number: 7,000

My Number: _____

My Score: _____

4. ☐☐☐☐

Target Number: 8,001

My Number: _____

My Score: _____

5. ☐☐☐☐

Target Number: 9,972

My Number: _____

My Score: _____

<u>Place</u> <u>The</u> <u>Digits</u> - <u>A</u>

Mathematics teaching objectives:

   . Use place value concepts.

   . Practice subtracting 4-digit numbers.

Problem-solving skills pupils <u>might</u> use:

   . Guess and check.

   . Look for a pattern.

Materials needed:

   . One set of ten small cards numbered 0 to 9. See page 2   for a master.

Comments and suggestions:

   . This is a whole class game-type activity. Space is provided on the work-sheet for five games. For each game,

     1. call pupils' attention to the target number for that game.

     2. announce that the winner of the game is the person to create a number closest to the target number <u>without</u> <u>going</u> <u>over</u>.

     3. mix deck of ten cards well. Draw out <u>one</u> <u>card</u> <u>at</u> <u>a</u> <u>time</u>.

     4. as cards are drawn, announce the digits on each aloud. Pupils write the digits <u>as</u> they are announced, in spaces of their own choosing.

     5. When all spaces are filled, pupils subtract the number they have created from the target number to determine their score.

     6. if the answer is more than the target number, the pupil gets an automatic score of 1000.

   The winner is the player whose score for all the games is lowest.

   . Rather than find a score for all five games, each can be played separately with a score of zero given for answers more than the target answer.

PLACE THE DIGITS - B

Follow the directions your teacher gives.

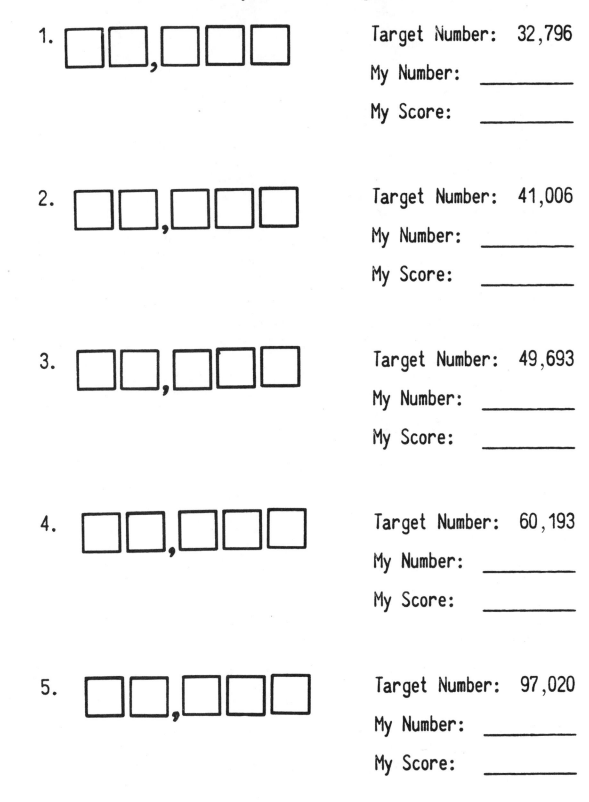

1. ⬜⬜,⬜⬜⬜

Target Number: 32,796

My Number: _____

My Score: _____

2. ⬜⬜,⬜⬜⬜

Target Number: 41,006

My Number: _____

My Score: _____

3. ⬜⬜,⬜⬜⬜

Target Number: 49,693

My Number: _____

My Score: _____

4. ⬜⬜,⬜⬜⬜

Target Number: 60,193

My Number: _____

My Score: _____

5. ⬜⬜,⬜⬜⬜

Target Number: 97,020

My Number: _____

My Score: _____

Place The Digits - B

Mathematics teaching objectives:

. Use place value concepts.

. Practice subtracting 5-digit numbers.

Problem-solving skills pupils <u>might</u> use:

. Guess and check.

. Look for a pattern.

Materials needed:

. One set of ten small cards numbered 0 to 9.   See page 2   for a master.

Comments and suggestions:

. This is a whole class game-type activity. Space is provided on the worksheet for five games. For each game,

1. call pupils' attention to the target number for that game.

2. announce that the winner of the game is the person to create a number closest to the target number <u>without going over</u>.

3. mix deck of ten cards well. Draw out <u>one card at a time</u>.

4. as cards are drawn, announce the digits on each aloud. Pupils write the digits <u>as</u> they are announced, in spaces of their own choosing.

5. When all spaces are filled, pupils subtract the number they have created from the target number to determine their score.

6. If the answer is more than the target number, the pupil gets an automatic score of 10,000.

The winner is the player whose score for all the games is lowest.

. Rather than find a score for all five games, each can be played separately with a score of zero given for answers more than the target answer.

PLACE THE DIGITS - C

Follow the directions your teacher gives.

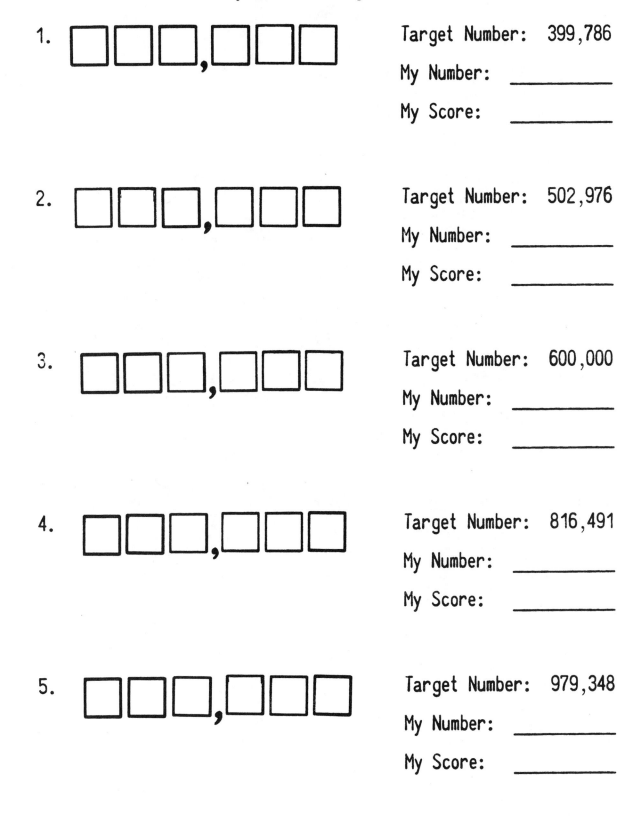

1. □□□,□□□

   Target Number: 399,786

   My Number: _____

   My Score: _____

2. □□□,□□□

   Target Number: 502,976

   My Number: _____

   My Score: _____

3. □□□,□□□

   Target Number: 600,000

   My Number: _____

   My Score: _____

4. □□□,□□□

   Target Number: 816,491

   My Number: _____

   My Score: _____

5. □□□,□□□

   Target Number: 979,348

   My Number: _____

   My Score: _____

Place The Digits - C

Mathematics teaching objectives:

. Use place value concepts.

. Practice subtracting 6-digit numbers.

Problem-solving skills pupils might use:

. Guess and check.

. Look for a pattern.

Materials needed:

. One set of ten small cards numbered 0 to 9. See page 2   for a master.

Comments and suggestions:

. This is a whole class game-type activity. Space is provided on the work-sheet for five games. For each game,

1. call pupils' attention to the target number for that game.

2. announce that the winner of the game is the person to create a number closest to the target number without going over.

3. mix deck of ten cards well. Draw out one card at a time.

4. as cards are drawn, announce the digits on each aloud. Pupils write the digits as they are announced, in spaces of their own choosing.

5. When all spaces are filled, pupils subtract the number they have created from the target number to determine their score.

6. If the answer is more than the target number, the pupil gets an automatic score of 100,000.

The winner is the player whose score for all the games is lowest.

. Rather than find a score for all five games, each can be played separately with a score of zero given for answers more than the target answer.

PLACE THE DIGITS - D

Follow the directions your teacher gives.

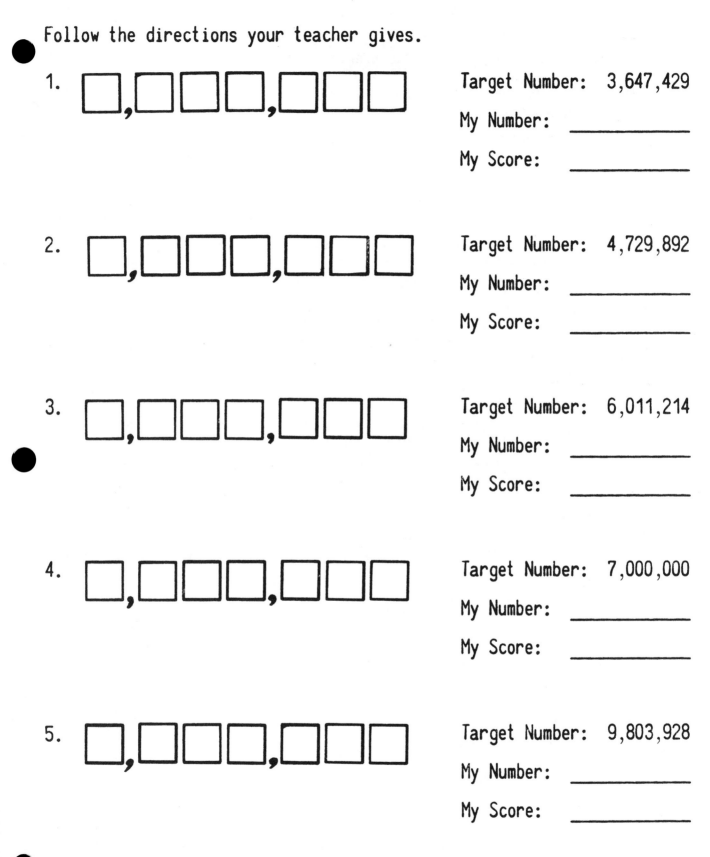

1. ☐,☐☐☐,☐☐☐   Target Number: 3,647,429

   My Number: _____

   My Score: _____

2. ☐,☐☐☐,☐☐☐   Target Number: 4,729,892

   My Number: _____

   My Score: _____

3. ☐,☐☐☐,☐☐☐   Target Number: 6,011,214

   My Number: _____

   My Score: _____

4. ☐,☐☐☐,☐☐☐   Target Number: 7,000,000

   My Number: _____

   My Score: _____

5. ☐,☐☐☐,☐☐☐   Target Number: 9,803,928

   My Number: _____

   My Score: _____

Place The Digits - D

Mathematics teaching objectives:

. Use place value concepts.

. Practice subtracting 7-digit numbers.

Problem-solving skills pupils might use:

. Guess and check.

. Look for a pattern.

Materials needed:

. One set of ten small cards numbered 0 to 9. See page 2   for a master.

Comments and suggestions:

. This is a whole class game-type activity. Space is provided on the work-sheet for five games. For each game,

    1. call pupils' attention to the target number for that game.

    2. announce that the winner of the game is the person to create a number closest to the target number without going over.

    3. mix deck of ten cards well. Draw out one card at a time.

    4. as cards are drawn, announce the digits on each aloud. Pupils write the digits as they are announced, in spaces of their own choosing.

    5. When all spaces are filled, pupils subtract the number they have created from the target number to determine their score.

    6. If the answer is more than the target number, the pupil gets an automatic score of 1,000,000.

The winner is the player whose score for all the games is lowest.

. Rather than find a score for all five games, each can be played separately with a score of zero given for answers more than the target answer.

DIGIT DEAL - A

NEEDED: Digit cards 1 - 9
          2 players

1. Mix the cards. Deal 3 cards to each player. Write the digits
    each of you received.

    Player 1 _____ _____ _____

    Player 2 _____ _____ _____

2. Each player:

    . use all three of your digits, once each.
    . make the best answers you can for each statement below
      (some may be impossible). Score one point for the player
      with the best answer.

		Player 1	Player 2	Best Answer
1.	Largest possible number			
2.	Smallest possible number			
3.	Number closest to 500			
4.	Largest even number			
5.	Smallest odd number			
6.	Even number closest to 400			
7.	Odd number closest to 300			
8.	Largest number between 350 and 450			
9.	Smallest number between 620 and 720			
10.	Smallest odd number between 710 and 810			

Digit Deal - A

Mathematics teaching objectives:

. Practice place value skills (3-digit numbers).

. Review odd, even, largest, smallest, between.

Problem-solving skills pupils might use:

. Guess and check.

. Break a problem into parts.

. Reason from what you already know.

Materials needed:

. Nine digit cards marked 1-9 (pattern on page 2)

. Transparency of pupil page (optional)

Comments and suggestions:

. Pupils need to understand the directions to the activity prior to forming partnerships to play the game. You might want to make a transparency of the pupil page and play a sample game with the whole class, one side of the room against the other side of the room.

. Pupils who finish ahead of others can use their own paper and play additional games.

Answers:

Answers will vary, depending upon which cards are dealt to each player. A sample is shown below.

Player 1: __2__ __9__ __3__   Player 2: __1__ __8__ __4__

	Player 1	Player 2	Best Answer
1.	932	841	Player 1
2.	239	148	Player 2
3.	392	481	Player 2
4.	932	814	Player 1
5.	239	481	Player 1
6.	392	418	Player 1
7.	293	481	Player 1
8.	392	418	Player 2
9.	not possible	not possible	_____
10.	not possible	not possible	_____

DIGIT DEAL - B

NEEDED: Digit cards 1-9
2 players

1. Mix the cards. Deal 4 cards to each player. Write the digits each of you received.

   Player 1 ____ ____ ____ ____

   Player 2 ____ ____ ____ ____

2. Each player:

   . use <u>all</u> <u>four</u> <u>of</u> <u>your</u> <u>digits</u>, <u>once</u> <u>each</u>.
   . make the best answers you can for each statement below (some may be impossible). Score one point for the player with the best answer.

		Player 1	Player 2	Best Answer
1.	Largest possible number			
2.	Smallest possible number			
3.	Number closest to 5,000			
4.	Largest even number			
5.	Smallest odd number			
6.	Even number closest to 4,000			
7.	Odd number closest to 3,000			
8.	Largest number between 3,500 and 4,500			
9.	Smallest number between 6,200 and 7,200			
10.	Smallest odd number between 7,100 and 8,100			

<u>Digit</u> <u>Deal</u> - <u>B</u>

Mathematics teaching objectives:

. Practice place value skills (4-digit numbers).

. Review odd, even, largest, smallest, between.

Problem-solving skills pupils <u>might</u> use:

. Guess and check.

. Break a problem into parts.

. Reason from what you already know.

Materials needed:

. Nine digit cards marked 1-9 (see page 2)

. Transparency of pupil page (optional)

Comments and suggestions:

. Pupils need to understand the directions to the activity prior to forming
partnerships to play the game. You might want to make a transparency
of the pupil page and play a sample game with the whole class,
one side of the room against the other side of the room.

. Pupils who finish ahead of others can use their own paper and play
additional games.

Answers:

Answers will vary, depending upon which cards are dealt to each player. A
sample is shown below.

Player 1: <u>6</u> <u>2</u> <u>4</u> <u>9</u>   Player 2: <u>8</u> <u>1</u> <u>7</u> <u>5</u>

	Player 1	Player 2	Best Answer
1.	9642	8751	Player 1
2.	2469	1578	Player 2
3.	4962	5178	Player 1
4.	9642	7518	Player 1
5.	2469	1587	Player 2
6.	4296	5178	Player 1
7.	2649	1857	Player 1
8.	4296	none possible	Player 1
9.	6246	7158	Player 1
10.	none possible	7185	Player 2

DIGIT DEAL - C

NEEDED: Digit cards 0 - 9
          2 players

1. Mix the cards. Deal 5 cards to each player. Write the digits
    each of you received.

    Player 1   ___ ___ ___ ___ ___

    Player 2   ___ ___ ___ ___ ___

2. Each player:

    . use all five of your digits, once each.
    . make the best answers you can for each statement below
       (some may be impossible). Score one point for the player
       with the best answer.

		Player 1	Player 2	Best Answer
1.	Largest possible number			
2.	Smallest possible number			
3.	Number closest to 50,000			
4.	Largest even number less than 75,000			
5.	Largest odd number less than 85,000			
6.	Even number closest to 40,000			
7.	Odd number closest to 30,000			
8.	Largest number between 25,000 and 35,000			
9.	Smallest number between 62,000 and 72,000			
10.	Smallest odd number between 18,200 and 19,200			

Digit Deal - C

Mathematics teaching objectives:

. Practice place value skills (5-digit numbers).

. Review odd, even, largest, smallest, between.

Problem-solving skills pupils might use:

. Guess and check.

. Break a problem into parts.

. Reason from what you already know.

Materials needed:

. Ten digit cards, marked 0-9 (see page 2)

. Transparency of pupil page (optional)

Comments and suggestions:

. Pupils need to understand the directions to the activity prior to forming partnerships to play the game. You might want to make a transparency of the pupil page and play a sample game with the whole class, one side of the room against the other side of the room.

. Pupils who finish ahead of others can use their own paper and play additional games.

Answers:

Answers will vary, depending upon which cards each player receives. A sample is shown below.

Player 1: __6__ __2__ __5__ __4__ __9__   Player 2: __7__ __3__ __8__ __0__ __1__

	Player 1	Player 2	Best Answer
1.	96,542	87,310	Player 1
2.	24,569	01,378	Player 2
3.	49,652	38,710	Player 1
4.	69,542	73,810	Player 2
5.	69,425	83,701	Player 2
6.	42,596	38,710	Player 2
7.	29,645	30,187	Player 2
8.	29,654	31,870	Player 2
9.	62,459	70,138	Player 1
10.	not possible	18,307	Player 2

DIGIT ADDITION – A

Follow the directions your teacher gives.

Game 1
□ □
□ □
+ □ □

Target Sum: _116_

My Sum: ____

Score: ____

Game 2
□ □
□ □
+ □ □

Target Sum: _137_

My Sum: ____

Score: ____

Game 3
□ □
□ □
+ □ □

Target Sum: _159_

My Sum: ____

Score: ____

Game 4
□ □
□ □
+ □ □

Target Sum: _176_

My Sum: ____

Score: ____

<u>Digit Addition</u> - <u>A</u>

Mathematics teaching objectives:

. Practice adding three 2-digit numbers.

. Use place value concepts.

Problem-solving skills pupils <u>might</u> use:

. Guess and check.

. Look for a pattern.

Materials needed:

. One set of ten small cards, numbered 0 to 9 (see page 2   for a master)

Comments and suggestions:

. This is a whole class, game-type activity. Space is provided on the worksheet to play 4 games. For each game,

    1. call pupils' attention to the target number for that game.

    2. announce that the winner of the game is the person to create a problem
        whose answer is closest to the target <u>without going over</u>.

    3. mix deck of ten cards well. Draw out <u>one</u> <u>card</u> <u>at</u> <u>a</u> <u>time</u>.

    4. as cards are drawn, announce the digit on each aloud. Pupils write
        the digits, <u>as</u> <u>they</u> <u>are</u> <u>announced</u>, in spaces of their own choosing.

    5. when all spaces are filled, pupils solve the problem they have
        created. The answer to that problem (if lower than target number)
        is subtracted from the target number to determine pupil's score.

        If the answer is more than the target answer, the pupil gets an
        automatic score of 50.

  The winner is the player whose score for all the games is lowest.

. Rather than find a score for all four games, each can be played separately
  with a score of zero given for answers more than the target answer.

Answers:

Answers will vary.

DIGIT ADDITION - B

Follow the directions your teacher gives.

Game **1**

Target Sum: 1,245

My Sum: _____

Score: _____

Game 2

Target Sum: 1,416

My Sum: _____

Score: _____

Game 3

Target Sum: 1,672

My Sum: _____

Score: _____

Game 4

Target Sum: 1,800

My Sum: _____

Score: _____

Digit Addition - B

Mathematics teaching objectives:

- Practice adding three 3-digit numbers.
- Use place value concepts.

Problem-solving skills pupils might use:

- Guess and check.
- Look for a pattern.

Materials needed:

- One set of ten small cards numbered 0 to 9 (see page 2   for a master)

Comments and suggestions:

- This is a whole class, game-type activity. Space is provided on the worksheet for 4 games. For each game,

    1. call pupils' attention to the target number for that game.

    2. announce that the winner of the game is the person to create a problem whose answer is closest to the target without going over.

    3. mix deck of ten cards well. Draw out one card at a time.

    4. as cards are drawn, announce the digit on each aloud. Pupils write the digits, as they are announced, in spaces of their own choosing.

    5. when all spaces are filled, pupils solve the problem they have created. The answer to that problem (if lower than target number) is subtracted from the target number to determine pupil's score.

    If the answer is more than the target answer, the pupil gets an automatic score of 250.

  The winner is the player whose score for all the games is lowest.

- Rather than find a score for all four games, each can be played separately with a score of zero given for answers more than the target answer.

Answers:

Answers will vary.

DIGIT ADDITION - C

Follow the directions your teacher gives.

Game 1

Target Sum: _10,248_

My Sum: _____

Score: _____

Game 2

Target Sum: _12,640_

My Sum: _____

Score: _____

Game 3

Target Sum: _15,308_

My Sum: _____

Score: _____

Game 4

Target Sum: _18,500_

My Sum: _____

Score: _____

Digit Addition - C

Mathematics teaching objectives:

. Practice adding three 4-digit numbers.

. Use place value concepts.

Problem-solving skills pupils might use:

. Guess and check.

. Look for a pattern.

Materials needed:

. One set of ten small cards, numbered 0 to 9 (see page 2 for a pattern)

Comments and suggestions:

. This is a whole class game-type activity. Space is provided on the worksheet for 4 games. For each game,

1. call pupils' attention to the target number for that game.

2. announce that the winner of the game is the person to create a problem whose answer is closest to the target without going over.

3. mix deck of ten cards well. Draw out one card at a time.

4. as cards are drawn, announce the digit on each aloud. Pupils write the digits, as they are announced, in spaces of their own choosing. Pupils will write each of the first two digits drawn in two spaces in order to fill all twelve spaces.

5. when all spaces are filled, pupils solve the problem they have created. The answer to that problem (if lower than target number) is subtracted from the target number to determine pupil's score.

If the answer is more than the target answer, the pupil gets an automatic score of 500.

The winner is the player whose score for all the games is lowest.

. Rather than find a score for all four games, each can be played separately with a score of zero given for answers more than the target answer.

Answers:

Answers will vary.

DIGIT SUBTRACTION - A

Follow the direction your teacher gives.

Game 1

☐ ☐
− ☐ ☐
_____

Target Difference: _10_

My Difference: _____

Score: _____

Game 2

☐ ☐
− ☐ ☐
_____

Target Difference: _25_

My Difference: _____

Score: _____

Game 3

☐ ☐
− ☐ ☐
_____

Target Difference: _30_

My Difference: _____

Score: _____

Game 4

☐ ☐
− ☐ ☐
_____

Target Difference: _45_

My Difference: _____

Score: _____

Game 5

☐ ☐
− ☐ ☐
_____

Target Difference: _60_

My Difference: _____

Score: _____

Digit Subtraction - A

Mathematics teaching objectives:

- Practice 2-digit subtraction problems.
- Use place value concepts.

Problem-solving skills pupils might use:

- Guess and check.
- Look for a pattern.

Materials needed:

- One set of ten small cards, numbered 0 to 9 (see page 2   for a master)

Comments and suggestions:

- This is a whole class game-type activity. Space is provided on the work-sheet for five games. For each game,

  1. call pupils' attention to the target number for that game.

  2. announce that the winner of the game is the person to create a problem whose answer is closest to the target without going over.

  3. mix deck of ten cards well. Draw out one card at a time.

  4. as cards are drawn, announce the digit on each aloud. Pupils write the digits, as they are announced, in spaces of their own choosing.

  5. when all spaces are filled, pupils solve the problem they have created. The answer to that problem (if lower than target number) is subtracted from the target number to determine pupil's score.

     If the answer is more than the target answer, the pupil gets an automatic score of 50.

  The winner is the player whose score for all the games is lowest.

- Rather than find a score for all five games, each can be played separately with a score of zero given for answers more than the target answer.

Answers:

Answers will vary.

DIGIT SUBTRACTION - B

Follow the directions your teacher gives.

Game **1**

Target **Difference:** _115_

My **Difference:** _____

Score: _____

Game **2**

Target **Difference:** _200_

My **Difference:** _____

Score: _____

Game **3**

Target **Difference:** _300_

My **Difference:** _____

Score: _____

Game **4**

Target **Difference:** _450_

My **Difference:** _____

Score: _____

Game **5**

Target **Difference:** _600_

My **Difference:** _____

Score: _____

© PSM 82

Digit Subtraction - B

Mathematics teaching objectives:

. Practice 3-digit subtraction problems.

. Use place value concepts.

Problem-solving skills pupils might use:

. Guess and check.

. Look for a pattern.

Materials needed:

. One set of ten small cards numbered 0 to 9 (see page 2 for a master)

Comments and suggestions:

. This is a whole class game-type activity. Space is provided on the
worksheet for five games. For each game,

1. call pupils' attention to the target number for that game.

2. announce that the winner of the game is the person to create a
problem whose answer is closest to the target without going over.

3. mix deck of ten cards well. Draw out one card at a time.

4. as cards are drawn, announce the digit on each aloud. Pupils write
the digits, as they are announced, in spaces of their own choosing.

5. when all spaces are filled, pupils solve the problem they have
created. The answer to that problem (if lower than target number)
is subtracted from the target number to determine pupil's score.

If the answer is more than the target answer, the pupil gets an
automatic score of 100.

The winner is the player whose score for all the games is lowest.

. Rather than find a score for all five games, each can be played separately
with a score of zero given for answers more than the target answer.

Answers:

Answers will vary.

DIGIT SUBTRACTION - C

Follow the directions your teacher gives.

Game 1

☐ ☐ ☐ ☐
− ☐ ☐ ☐ ☐
_____

Target Difference: __1,123__

My Difference: _____

Score: _____

Game 2

☐ ☐ ☐ ☐
− ☐ ☐ ☐ ☐
_____

Target Difference: __2,500__

My Difference: _____

Score: _____

Game 3

☐ ☐ ☐ ☐
− ☐ ☐ ☐ ☐
_____

Target Difference: __3,899__

My Difference: _____

Score: _____

Game 4

☐ ☐ ☐ ☐
− ☐ ☐ ☐ ☐
_____

Target Difference: __5,001__

My Difference: _____

Score: _____

Game 5

☐ ☐ ☐ ☐
− ☐ ☐ ☐ ☐
_____

Target Difference: __6,000__

My Difference: _____

Score: _____

© PSM 82

Digit Subtraction - C

Mathematics teaching objectives:

· Practice 4-digit subtraction problems.

· Use place value concepts.

Problem-solving skills pupils might use:

· Guess and check.

· Look for a pattern.

Materials needed:

· One set of ten small cards numbered 0 to 9 (see page 2 for a master)

Comments and suggestions:

· This is a whole class game-type activity. Space is provided on the work-sheet for five games. For each game,

1. call pupils' attention to the target number for that game.

2. announce that the winner of the game is the person to create a problem whose answer is closest to the target without going over.

3. mix deck of ten cards well. Draw out one card at a time.

4. as cards are drawn, announce the digit on each aloud. Pupils write the digits, as they are announced, in spaces of their own choosing.

5. when all spaces are filled, pupils solve the problem they have created. The answer to that problem (if lower than target number) is subtracted from the target number to determine pupil's score.

If the answer is more than the target answer, the pupil gets an automatic score of 200.

The winner is the player whose score for all the games is lowest.

· Rather than find a score for all five games, each can be played separately with a score of zero given for answers more than the target answer.

Answers:

Answers will vary.

MAKE EACH SUM DIFFERENT - A

In each problem below use any
four of these digits, once each.

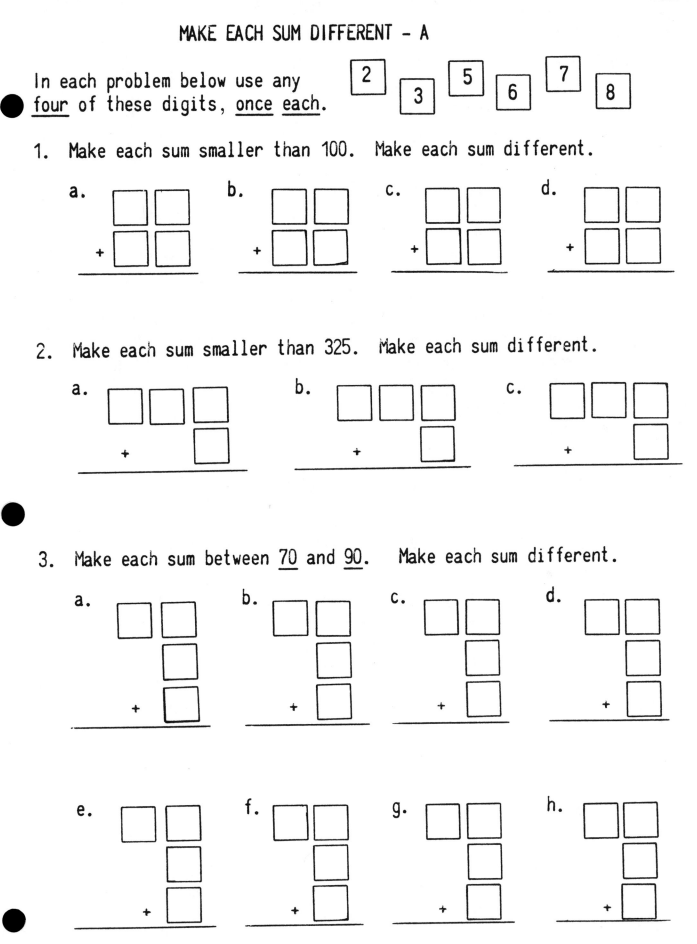

1. Make each sum smaller than 100. Make each sum different.

   a.   b.   c.   d.

2. Make each sum smaller than 325. Make each sum different.

   a.   b.   c.

3. Make each sum between 70 and 90. Make each sum different.

   a.   b.   c.   d.

   e.   f.   g.   h.

Make Each Sum Different - A

Mathematics teaching objectives:

- Practice 1-, 2-, and 3-digit addition.
- Use place value concepts

Problem-solving skills pupils might use:

- Make an organized list.
- Use previously-acquired knowledge.
- Look for a pattern.
- Guess and check.

Materials needed:

- None

Comments and suggestions:

- Discuss directions. Do part 1 as a class. Have pupils complete the remainder of the page on their own or by working with a partner.
- When pupils have completed the activity, have them pair up and check each other's work. Discuss any strategies pupils used to find correct solutions quickly.

Answers:

1. Answers will vary. Accept any four answers smaller than 100 that meet the requirements of the activity.

2. Answers will vary. Accept any four answers smaller than 325 that meet the requirements of the activity.

3. Answers will vary. Accept any eight answers between 70 and 90 that meet the requirements of the activity.

MAKE EACH SUM DIFFERENT - B

In each problem below use any six of these digits, once each.

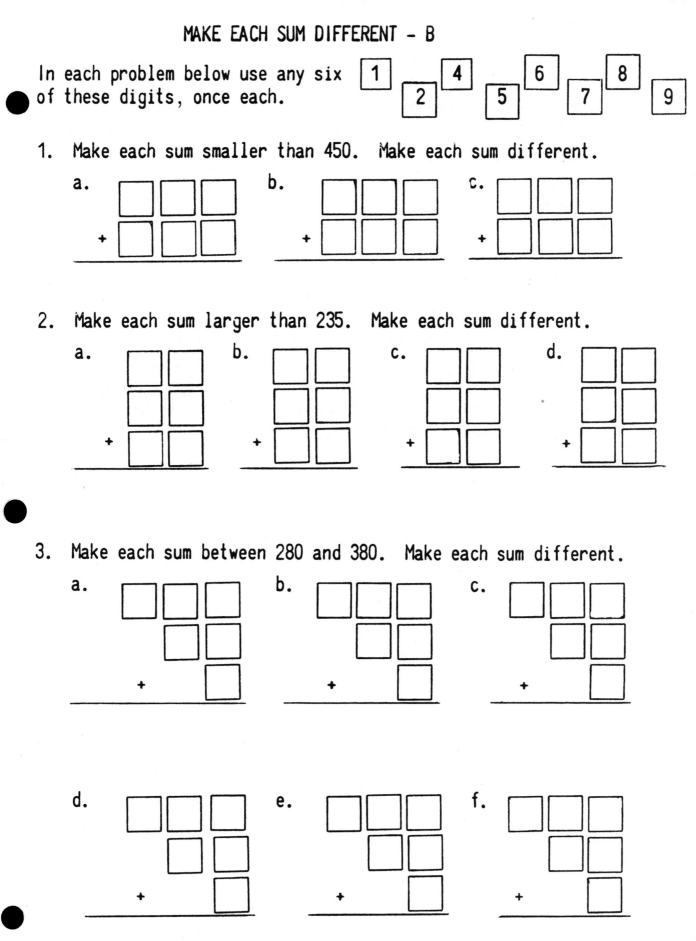

1. Make each sum smaller than 450. Make each sum different.

   a.

   b.

   c.

2. Make each sum larger than 235. Make each sum different.

   a.

   b.

   c.

   d.

3. Make each sum between 280 and 380. Make each sum different.

   a.

   b.

   c.

   d.

   e.

   f.

Make Each Sum Different - B

Mathematics teaching objectives:

- Practice 1-, 2-, and 3-digit addition.
- Use place value concepts.

Problem-solving skills pupils <u>might</u> use:

- Make an organized list.
- Use previously-acquired knowledge.
- Look for a pattern.
- Guess and check.

Materials needed:

- None

Comments and suggestions:

- Discuss directions. Do part 1 as a class. Have pupils complete the remainder of the page on their own or by working with a partner.
- When pupils have completed the activity, have them pair up and check each other's work. Discuss any strategies pupils used to find correct solutions quickly.

Answers:

Answers will vary. Accept any answers that meet the requirements of the activity.

DIFFERENT SUMS - A

In each problem below use all five of these digits, once each.

Make each answer different.

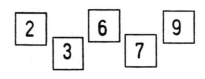

a.
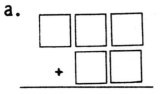

b.
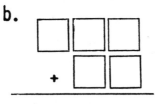

c.
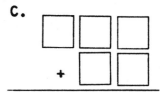

d.
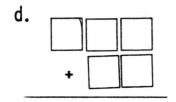

e.
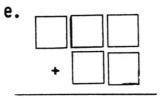

f.
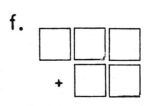

g.
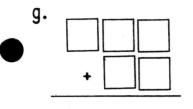

h.
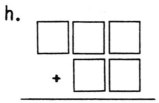

i.
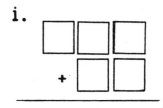

j.
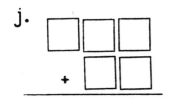

k.
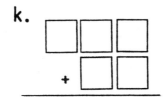

l.
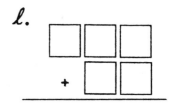

Different Sums - A

Mathematics teaching objectives:

. Practice adding 2- and 3-digit numbers.

. Use place value concepts.

Problem-solving skills pupils might use:

. Guess and check.

. Look for a pattern.

. Use an organized list.

Materials needed:

. Calculators for checking answers (optional)

Comments and suggestions:

. Discuss directions. Have pupils complete the page on their own or by working with a partner.

. Since there are a large number of possible correct answers, you may wish to have pupils pair up and check each other's answers. Calculators are helpful for this purpose if you have them available.

Answers:

Answers will vary. A large number of correct answers are possible.

DIFFERENT SUMS - B

1. In each problem below, use all six of these digits, once each. Make each answer different.

1		5		7	
	3		6		9

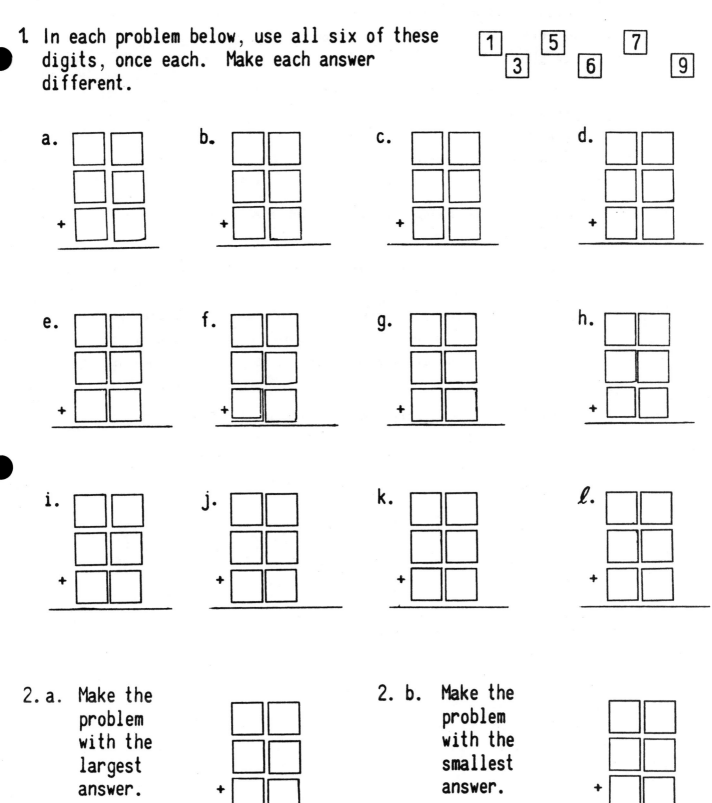

2. a. Make the problem with the largest answer.

2. b. Make the problem with the smallest answer.

Different Sums - B

Mathematics teaching objectives:

    . Practice adding three 2-digit numbers.

    . Use place value concepts.

Problem-solving skills pupils might use:

    . Guess and check.

    . Look for a pattern.

    . Use an organized list.

Materials needed:

    . None (Calculators optional for checking answers.)

Comments and suggestions:

    . Discuss directions. Have pupils complete the page on their own or by working with a partner.

    . Since there are a large number of possible correct answers, you may wish to have pupils pair up and check each other's answers. Calculators are helpful for this purpose if you have them available.

Answers:

    1. a-ℓ. Answers will vary. A large number of different answers are possible.

    2. a. $61 + 73 + 95 = 229$

         b. $16 + 37 + 59 = 112$

DIFFERENT DIFFERENCES - A

In each problem below use all four of
these digits, once each.
Make each problem different.

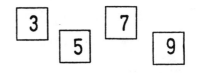

a.

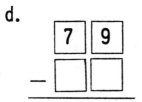

$$\begin{array}{r} 9\;7 \\ -\;3\;5 \\ \hline \end{array}$$

b.

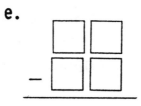

$$\begin{array}{r} 9\;7 \\ -\;5\;3 \\ \hline \end{array}$$

c.

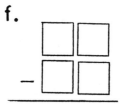

$$\begin{array}{r} 7\;9 \\ -\;3\;\square \\ \hline \end{array}$$

d.

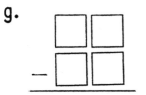

$$\begin{array}{r} 7\;9 \\ -\;\square\;\square \\ \hline \end{array}$$

e.

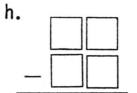

f.

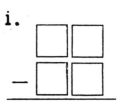

g.

h.

i.

j.

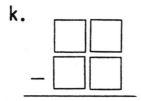

k.

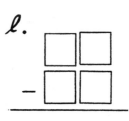

l.

Different Differences - A

Mathematics teaching objectives:

· Practice subtracting two 2-digit numbers.

· Use place value concepts.

Problem-solving skills pupils might use:

· Guess and check.

· Look for a pattern.

· Use an organized list.

Materials needed:

· None (Calculators optional for checking answers.)

Comments and suggestions:

· Discuss directions. Have pupils complete the page on their own or by working with a partner.

· Since there are a fairly large number of correct answers that may appear in any order, you may wish to have pupils pair up and check each other's answers. Calculators are helpful for this purpose if you have them available.

Answers:

a. 62   b. 44   c.   79   d.   79
                                 - 35   - 53
                                   44   26

e-*l.* Accept these problems and answers in any order:

95	95	93	93	75	73	57	59
- 37	- 73	- 75	- 57	- 39	- 59	- 39	- 37
58	22	18	36	36	14	18	22

DIFFERENT DIFFERENCES - B

In each problem below use all five of these digits, once each.

Make each answer different.

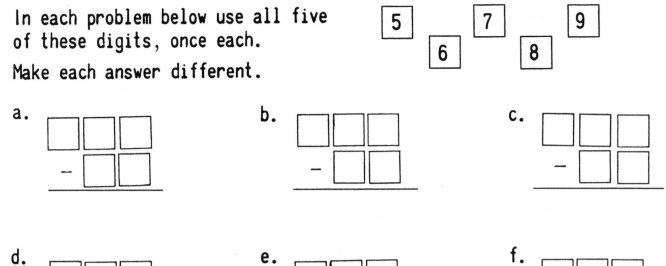

a.
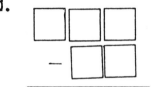

b.
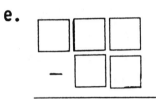

c.
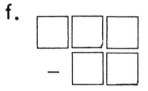

d.
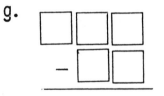

e.
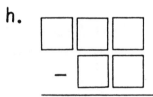

f.
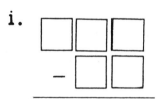

g.
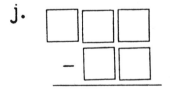

h.
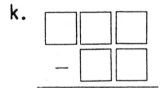

i.
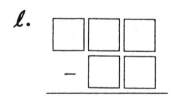

j.

k.

l.

m.

n.
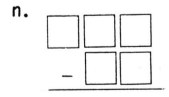

o.
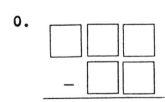

<u>Different Differences</u> - <u>B</u>

Mathematics teaching objectives:

. Practice subtracting 2-digit numbers from 3-digit numbers.

. Use place value concepts.

Problem-solving skills pupils <u>might</u> use:

. Guess and check.

. Look for a pattern.

. Use an organized list.

Materials needed:

. None (Calculators optional for use in checking answers.)

Comments and suggestions:

. Discuss directions. Have pupils complete the page on their own or by working with a partner.

. Since there are a fairly large number of correct answers that may appear in any order, you may wish to have pupils pair up and check each other's answers. Calculators are helpful for this purpose if you have them available.

Answers:

Answers will vary. A large number of correct answers are possible.

As a class you might wish to compile a complete listing.

CALCULATORS AND CARDS

1. Use any two numbers on the cards.
   Complete each addition problem below.
   Check your work with a calculator.

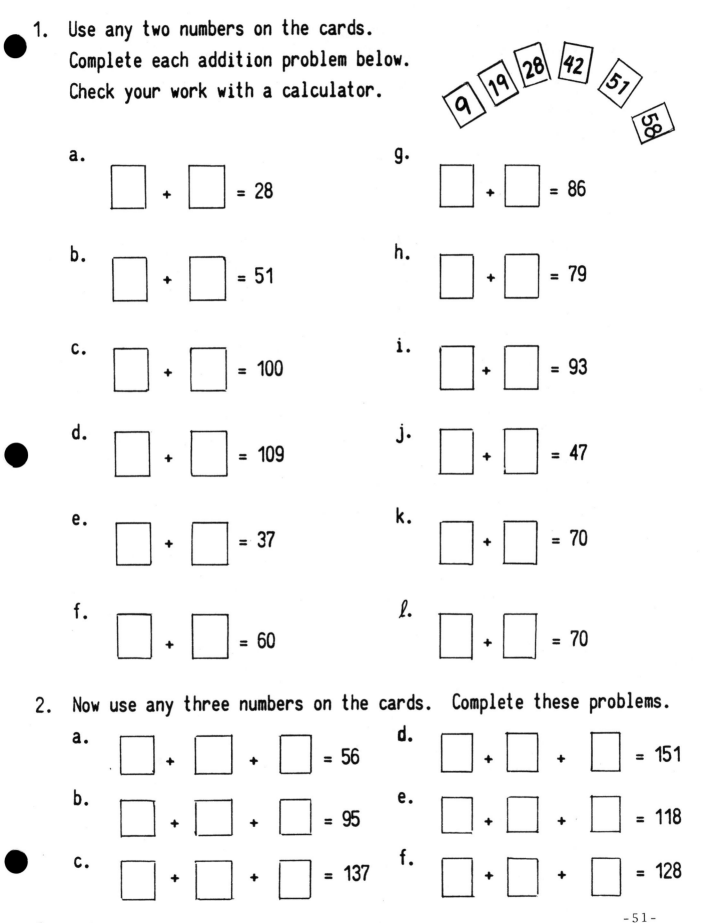

a. ☐ + ☐ = 28

b. ☐ + ☐ = 51

c. ☐ + ☐ = 100

d. ☐ + ☐ = 109

e. ☐ + ☐ = 37

f. ☐ + ☐ = 60

g. ☐ + ☐ = 86

h. ☐ + ☐ = 79

i. ☐ + ☐ = 93

j. ☐ + ☐ = 47

k. ☐ + ☐ = 70

ℓ. ☐ + ☐ = 70

Cards: 9 19 28 42 51 58

2. Now use any three numbers on the cards. Complete these problems.

a. ☐ + ☐ + ☐ = 56

b. ☐ + ☐ + ☐ = 95

c. ☐ + ☐ + ☐ = 137

d. ☐ + ☐ + ☐ = 151

e. ☐ + ☐ + ☐ = 118

f. ☐ + ☐ + ☐ = 128

© PSM 81

Calculators and Cards

Mathematics teaching objectives:

. Mentally add two-digit numbers (2 or 3 addends).

. Use place value concepts to make reasonable estimates.

Problem-solving skills pupils might use:

. Guess and check.

. Make reasonable estimates.

Materials needed:

. One calculator for each pair of pupils (optional)

Comments and suggestions:

. Work a few examples as a class, then have pupils pair up to complete the page.

Answers:

1. a. 9 + 19   g. 58 + 28
    b. 42 + 9   h. 28 + 51
    c. 58 + 42   i. 42 + 51
    d. 51 + 58   j. 19 + 28
    e. 28 + 9   k. 28 + 42 or 19 + 51
    f. 51 + 9   l. 28 + 42

2. a. 9 + 19 + 28   d. 42 + 51 + 58
    b. 19 + 28 + 58   e. 51 + 58 + 9
    c. 28 + 51 + 58   f. 51 + 58 + 19

CROSS SUMS - A

1. In each puzzle below
    . Use any of these numbers: 1, 2, 3, 4, 5, 6, 7, 8, 9.
    . Use a number only one time.
    . Fill in the circles. Make the sum of the numbers going across <u>the same</u> as the sum of the numbers going down.

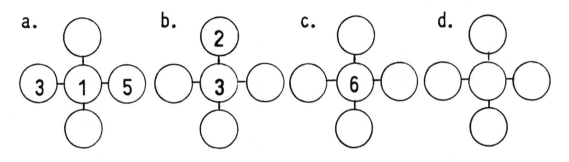

2. Fill in the circles so that the sum across is <u>one more</u> than the sum going down.

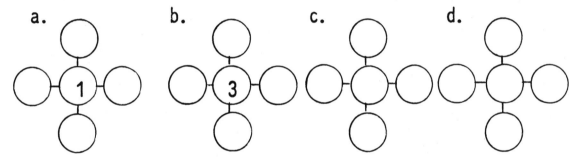

EXTENSION

Use the back of this page.
Make up your own "Cross Sum" puzzles.

PSM 81

-53-

Cross Sums - A

Mathematics teaching objectives:

. Practice basic addition facts.

. Recognize and use addition/subtraction relationships.

Problem-solving skills pupils might use:

. Guess and check.

. Eliminate possibilities.

Materials needed:

None.

Comments and suggestions:

. Work the examples in no. 1 as a class. Discuss the possibility of more than one right answer for some of the problems. As the problems are worked together, encourage a search for, and proof of, all possible solutions.

. When most pupils have completed the page, discuss solutions and share problems pupils have made up for the extension activity.

Answers:

1. a.

b-d. Answers will vary.

2. a-d. Answers will vary.

WIGWAM PUZZLES - A

1. Here are some
    2-floor wigwams.

    Finish these 2-floor
    wigwams.

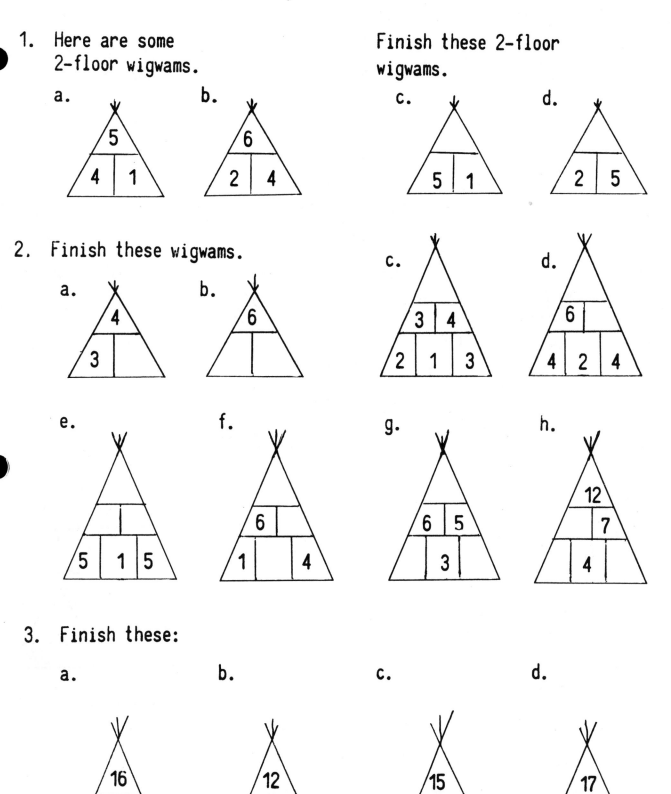

2. Finish these wigwams.

3. Finish these:

Wigwam Puzzles - A

Mathematics teaching objectives:

. Practice addition and subtraction skills.

. Use mental arithmetic.

Problem-solving skills pupils might use:

. Guess and check.

. Work backwards.

. Eliminate possibilities.

Materials needed:

. None

Comments and suggestions:

. Work the problems in part 1 as a class. Be sure pupils understand how the "upper floor" numbers are determined. Have pupils complete the remaining problems on their own.

. Pupils who have difficulty with (b) in no. 3 may need encouragement to guess and check, "working backwards" from the top floor to the bottom floor.

Answers:

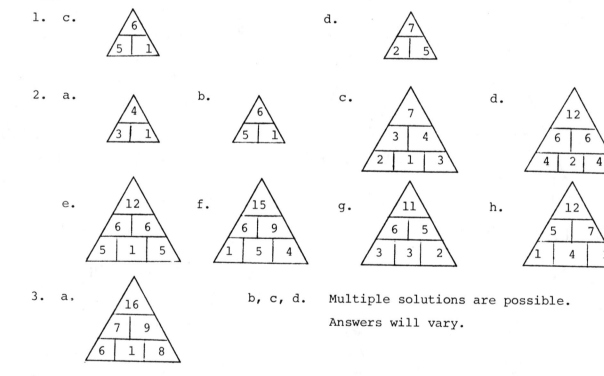

1. c.   6 / 5 | 1

    d.   7 / 2 | 5

2. a.   4 / 3 | 1

    b.   6 / 5 | 1

    c.   7 / 3 | 4 / 2 | 1 | 3

    d.   12 / 6 | 6 / 4 | 2 | 4

    e.   12 / 6 | 6 / 5 | 1 | 5

    f.   15 / 6 | 9 / 1 | 5 | 4

    g.   11 / 6 | 5 / 3 | 3 | 2

    h.   12 / 5 | 7 / 1 | 4 | 3

3. a.   16 / 7 | 9 / 6 | 1 | 8

    b, c, d.   Multiple solutions are possible. Answers will vary.

Extension:

Pupils who finish ahead of others can be asked to make up additional 3- or 4-floor wigwam puzzles for classmates to solve.

MAZES

Find a path through each maze that gives the sum at the end. Some mazes have more than one correct path.

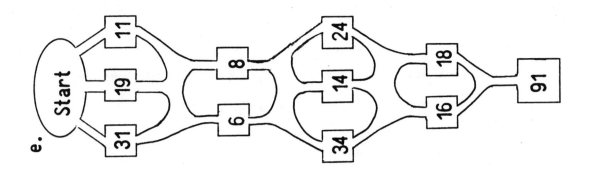

e.

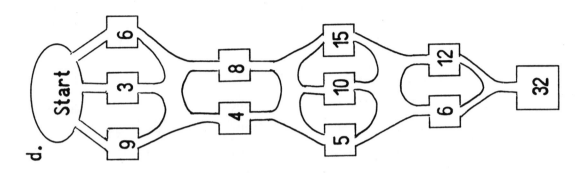

d.

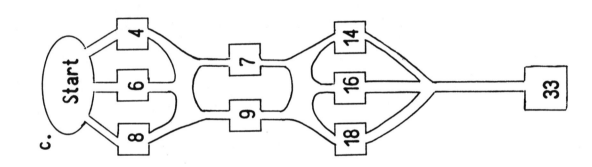

c.

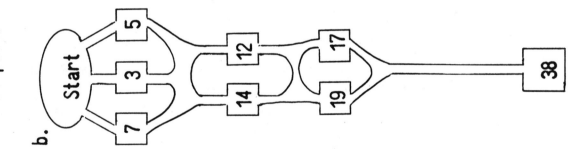

b.

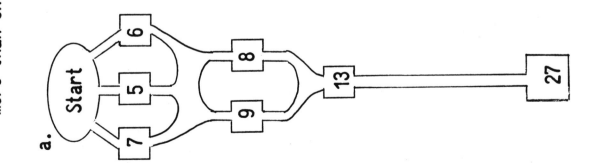

a.

Mazes

Mathematics teaching objective:

    . Practice addition and subtraction of whole numbers.

Problem-solving skills pupils <u>might</u> use:

    . Guess and check.

    . Work backwards.

    . Eliminate possibilities.

Materials needed:

    . None

Comments and suggestions:

    . Work the first example together as a class. Find <u>both</u> correct paths. Remind pupils that other mazes on this page may have more than one correct answer, then have pupils complete the page on their own. (If you wish, challenge pupils to find <u>all</u> possible solutions.)

    . Discuss solutions as a class. If any pupils have completed the extension activity, ask them to share the puzzles they created.

Answers:

    a. 5 + 9 + 13   or   6 + 8 + 13

    b. 5 + 14 + 19   or 7 + 14 + 17   or 7 + 12 + 19

    c. 6 + 9 + 18   or   8 + 7 + 18   or   8 + 9 + 16

    d. 6 + 4 + 10 + 12   or   3 + 8 + 15 + 6

    e. 31 + 8 + 34 + 18

Extension:

Have pupils who complete the page ahead of others make up their own maze problems for other pupils to solve.

BANK ON IT

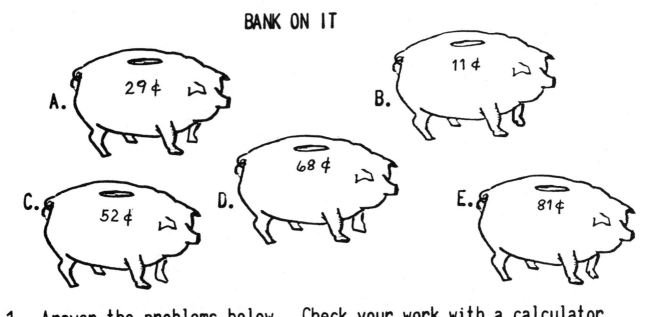

A. 29¢ B. 11¢ C. 52¢ D. 68¢ E. 81¢

1. Answer the problems below. Check your work with a calculator.

   a. Which two banks contain 40¢ in all? ____ and ____

   b. Which two banks contain 63¢ in all? ____ and ____

   c. Which two banks contain 92¢ in all? ____ and ____

   d. Which two banks contain 97¢ in all? ____ and ____

   e. Which two banks contain $1.33 in all? ____ and ____

   f. Which <u>three</u> banks contain 92¢ in all? ____ , ____ and ____

   g. Which <u>three</u> banks contain $1.49 in all? ____ , ____ and ____

2. Make up other problems about the banks.
   Write the problems and answers on the back of this paper.

Bank On It

Mathematics teaching objectives:

 . Mentally add two or three two-digit numbers.

 . Use place value concepts to make reasonable estimates.

Problem-solving skills pupils might use:

 . Guess and check.

 . Make reasonable estimates.

 . Eliminate possibilities.

Materials needed:

 . None

Comments and suggestions:

 . Work several problems together as a class and then have pupils complete the page on their own or by working with a partner.

 . Allow time for pupils to share the problems they made up for part 2.

Answers:

1. a. 29(A) and 11(B)

   b. 52(C) and 11(B)

   c. 81(E) and 11(B)

   d. 68(D) and 29(A)

   e. 81(E) and 52(C)

   f. 52(C), 29(A), and 11(B)

   g. 29(A), 68(D), and 52(C)

2. Answers will vary.

COIN PROBLEMS - A

1. Use 3 coins.
    Make 16¢.
    ____dimes ____nickels ____pennies

2. Use 4 coins.
    Make 21¢.
    ____dimes ____nickels ____pennies

3. Use 4 coins.
    Make 26¢.
    ____dimes ____nickels ____pennies

4. Use 5 coins.
    Make 31¢.
    ____dimes ____nickels ____pennies

5. Find ways to make 24¢. Finish the chart below.

	Dimes	Nickels	Pennies
a.	2	0	
b.	1	2	
c.	1	1	
d.	1	0	
e.	0	4	
f.	0		
g.	0		
h.	0		
i.	0		

Coin Problems - A

Mathematics teaching objectives:

- Practice with mental addition.
- Practice naming and using coin values (pennies, nickels, dimes).

Problem-solving skills pupils might use:

- Guess and check.
- Make a systematic list.
- Work backwards.

Materials needed:

- None

Comments and suggestions:

- Discuss nos.1 and 2 as a class, perhaps using real coins to show answers. Have pupils complete the remainder of the page on their own or by working with a partner.
- Discuss and compare results when pupils have completed the page. In particular, compare the ways pupils organized the list used to solve no. 5. They will notice and want to discuss the various patterns evident in the lists.

Answers:

1. 1 dime, 1 nickel, 1 penny

2. 1 dime, 2 nickels, 1 penny

3. 2 dimes, 1 nickel, 1 penny

4. 2 dimes, 2 nickels, 1 penny

5.

	dimes	nickels	pennies
a.	2	0	4
b.	1	2	4
c.	1	1	9
d.	1	0	14
e.	0	4	4
f.	0	3	9
g.	0	2	14
h.	0	1	19
i.	0	0	24

Extension:

Show all the ways to make 50¢ with just dimes and/or nickels.

COIN PROBLEMS - B

1. Use 3 coins. Make 25¢.
    _____quarters _____dimes _____nickels _____pennies

2. Use 3 coins. Make 45¢.
    _____quarters _____dimes _____nickels _____pennies

3. Use 5 coins. Make 30¢.
    _____quarters _____dimes _____nickels _____pennies

4. Use 6 coins. Make 30¢.
    _____quarters _____dimes _____nickels _____pennies

5. Use a total of four coins.
    What different amounts of money can you make?
    Finish the chart below. Find out.

	Dimes	Nickels	Pennies	Total
a.	4	0		40¢
b.	3	1		35¢
c.	3	0		31¢
d.	2	2		
e.	2	1		
f.	2			22¢
g.	1	3		
h.	1	2		
i.	1			17¢
j.	1			13¢
k.	0	4		
l.	0	3		
m.	0			
n.	0			
o.	0			

Coin Problems - B

Mathematics teaching objectives:

- Practice with mental addition.
- Practice naming and using coin values (pennies, nickels, dimes, quarters).

Problem-solving skills pupils _might_ use:

- Guess and check.
- Make a systematic list.
- Work backwards.

Materials needed:

- None

Comments and suggestions:

- Discuss and complete nos. 1 and 2 as a class, perhaps using real coins to show answers. Have pupils work the remainder of the page on their own or by working with a partner.
- Discuss and compare results when pupils have completed the page. In particular, compare the ways pupils organized the list to solve no. 5. They will notice and want to discuss the various patterns they recognize in the lists.

Answers:

1. 2 dimes, 1 nickel

2. 1 quarter, 2 dimes

3. 1 dime, 4 nickels

4. 1 quarter, 5 pennies

5.

	dimes	nickels	pennies	total
a.	4	0	0	40¢
b.	3	1	0	35¢
c.	3	0	1	31¢
d.	2	2	0	30¢
e.	2	1	1	26¢
f.	2	0	2	22¢
g.	1	3	0	25¢
h.	1	2	1	21¢
i.	1	1	2	17¢
j.	1	0	3	13¢
k.	0	4	0	20¢
ℓ.	0	3	1	16¢
m.	0	2	2	12¢
n.	0	1	3	8¢
o.	0	0	4	4¢

Extension:

Use a total of 5 coins (quarters, dimes, nickels and/or pennies are allowed). Find how many different amounts of money can be made.

MAKE 50 ¢

1. Make 50¢.   __4__ dimes   __1__ nickels   ____ pennies

2. Make 50¢.   __3__ dimes   __1__ nickels   ____ pennies

3. Make 50¢.   ____ dimes   ____ nickels   __25__ pennies

4. Find ways to make 50¢ using one quarter.
   Finish the chart below.

	quarters	dimes	nickels	pennies
a.	1	2	1	0
b.	1	2	0	
c.	1	1	3	
d.	1	1	2	
e.	1	1	1	
f.	1	1		
g.	1			
h.	1			
i.	1			
j.	1			
k.	1			
ℓ.	1			

Make 50¢

Mathematics teaching objectives:

. Practice mental addition using coin values (quarters, dimes, nickels, pennies).

Problem-solving skills pupils might use:

. Guess and check.
. Make an organized list.

Materials needed:

. None

Comments and suggestions:

. Work the first few problems as a class. Have pupils complete the remainder of the page on their own.
. Some pupils may need help organizing the list used in no. 4. Give individual assistance, as needed.

Answers:

1. 4 dimes, 1 nickel, 5 pennies

2. 3 dimes, 1 nickel, 15 pennies

3. 2 dimes, 1 nickel, 25 pennies,   or
    1 dime, 3 nickels, 25 pennies,   or
    0 dimes, 5 nickels, 25 pennies

4.

	quarters	dimes	nickels	pennies
a.	1	2	1	0
b.	1	2	0	5
c.	1	1	3	0
d.	1	1	2	5
e.	1	1	1	10
f.	1	1	0	15
g.	1	0	5	0
h.	1	0	4	5
i.	1	0	3	10
j.	1	0	2	15
k.	1	0	1	20
ℓ.	1	0	0	25

Extension:

Find ways to make 50¢ using quarters, dimes, and/or nickels (no pennies).

BUILD YOUR OWN BURGER

Price List For Bargain Burgers			
Plain bun	12¢	Onion	3¢
Sesame seed bun	14¢	Lettuce	4¢
Beef patty	8¢	American cheese	5¢
Pickle	1¢	Swiss cheese	6¢
Special sauce	2¢	Tomato	7¢

1. Use the price list above.
   Make a burger with plain bun,
   beef patty, and special sauce.

   Find its total cost. Record.

   plain bun ____¢
   beef patty ____¢
   special sauce ____¢
   total ____¢

2. Make a burger which costs
   25¢

   Record.

Item	Cost
_____	____¢
_____	____¢
_____	____¢
_____	____¢
_____	____¢
_____	____¢
total	____

3. How many different burgers can you make which each cost 30¢?
   Find out. Record your findings on the back of this page.

Build Your Own Burger

Mathematics teaching objectives:

. Use mental arithmetic.

. Practice addition and subtraction skills.

Problem-solving skills pupils might use:

. Make reasonable estimates.

. Guess and check.

. Work backwards.

. Make and use a systematic list.

Materials needed:

. None

Comments and suggestions:

. All burgers must have at least one beef patty.

. For activities 2 and 3 the class may want to decide whether to allow two or more of the same ingredients on one burger (2 pickles, for example).

. Be sure pupils list both the items and their prices when recording answers to activity 3.

. Obviously, the prices in this lesson are from a "make believe" store. After pupils complete the lesson, they might be interested in substituting more realistic prices.

Answers:

1. 22¢

2. Accept any of the following answers:

pb	pb	pb	pb	pb	pb	sb	sb	sb
bp	bp	bp	bp	bp	bp	bp	bp	bp
p	ss	ac	ss	p	p	o	ss	p
ℓ	o		ss	p	p		p	p
			p	p	o			p
			ss					

Talk about how many math problems (especially real world ones) have more than one right answer.

3. This problem has many right answers. Give pupils ample time to work on the problem independently. Then, as a class, compile a list of the various correct solutions found. It helps to organize this list in some way. For example, list all the solutions with plain buns; then list all the solutions with sesame seed buns. A letter code, such as used in the answer key for problem 2, is helpful in getting down ideas fast.

Extensions:

Using the price list, you can make up an unlimited number of story problems. Pupils, too, can make up and solve their own problems.

Use the toy store. Buy gifts for friends. The gifts can be the same.

1. Buy 2 things.
    Give clerk 10¢.
    Get 3¢ change.
    What did you buy?

    _____ + _____

2. Buy 2 things.
    Give clerk 10¢.
    Get 4¢ change.
    What did you buy?

    _____ + _____

3. Buy 3 things.
    Give clerk a dime.
    Get 4¢ change.
    What did you buy?

    _____ + _____ + _____

4. Buy 3 things.
    Give clerk 15¢.
    Get 4¢ change.
    What did you buy?

    _____ + _____ + _____

5. Buy 3 things.
    Give clerk a dime.
    Get no change.
    What did you buy?

    _____ + _____ + _____

    or _____ + _____ + _____

6. How many different ways can you
    spend 15¢ at this store?
    Record each way you find below.

<u>Smart Shopper</u>

Mathematics teaching objectives:

- . Practice basic addition and subtraction facts.
- . Practice naming the value of coins and making change (mentally).
- . Informally practice with 2-step story problems having "real world" settings.

Problem-solving skills pupils <u>might</u> use:

- . Guess and check.
- . Make reasonable estimates.
- . Work backwards.
- . Search for and be aware of other solutions.

Materials needed:

- . None

Comments and suggestions:

- . Discuss and complete no.1 together as a class, perhaps acting the problem out using real coins.
- . Pupils can complete the remainder of the page on their own or can work with a partner.
- . Actual coins or toy money might be helpful for pupils who find the activity difficult.
- . Have pupils compare their solutions with others in the class.

Answers:

1. ball and bat
2. ball and car
3. 3 balls
4. bat, ball, car
5. bus and 2 balls <u>or</u> 2 cars and a ball
6. 3 bats (5¢, 5¢, 5¢) <u>or</u> bat, car, bus (5¢, 4¢, 6¢) <u>or</u>
   bat, 5 balls (5¢, 2¢, 2¢, 2¢, 2¢, 2¢) <u>or</u>
   bat, bus, 2 balls (5¢, 6¢, 2¢, 2¢) <u>or</u>
   car, bat, 3 balls (5¢, 4¢, 2¢, 2¢, 2¢) <u>or</u>
   bat, 2 cars, 1 ball (5¢, 4¢, 4¢, 2¢)

Extension:

Pupils who finish the page successfully may be asked to make up their own "used toy store" problems.

MAKING A TALLY

> A tally is a useful way to collect and record information. Facts, when tallied, often show trends.

1. In grocery store ads, what digit do you think is used most? _____   least? _____

2. Find a full (or double) page grocery store advertisement in a newspaper. Record the name of the grocery store.

   _____

   Use the chart below to tally each digit used in the prices of the items in the ad.

0		5	
1		6	
2		7	
3		8	
4		9	

3. Write two conclusions you would make about grocery store ads.

CHALLENGE   Find the advertisement of another kind of store. Record the name of the store. _____

Predict the most and least used digits in the prices:
   most used digit _____   least used digit _____

Tally the information. Write about your results. Explain any differences or similarities you found between the two kinds of stores.

<u>Making A Tally</u>

Mathematics teaching objective:

. Use place value and money concepts in a consumer setting.

Problem-solving skills pupils <u>might</u> use:

. Make a systematic list (tally).

. Look for a pattern.

. Make predictions based upon data.

Materials needed:

. One full (or double) page grocery store advertisement for each <u>pair</u> of pupils.

Comments and suggestions:

. Pupils will be able to complete this activity with a minimum of teacher direction if they are familiar with how to make a tally. Review the use of a tally, then have pupils, working in pairs, finish the page.

. When most pupils have finished, discuss and compare results.

. Did pupils who picked the <u>same</u> ad get the same results?

. Did pupils who picked <u>different</u> ads get similar results?

Answers:

Answers will vary.

USING CLASSIFIED ADS

> When people want to sell (or buy) an item, they can place an advertisement in the classified ads.

1. Find the index to the classified ad section.
   In which section of the classified ads would you find
   . dogs for sale? _____
   . used boats for sale? _____
   . lost and found? _____
   . help wanted? _____
   . cameras for sale? _____

2. Look through the ads for a bike, T.V. set, musical instrument, or other item you might like to buy. Copy the ad you chose:

   _____
   _____
   _____

3. Find something in the classified ads that sells for
   . between $12 and $50 _____
   . between $75 and $125 _____
   . between $750 and $1250 _____
   . between $12,500 and $50,000 _____
   . over $100,000 _____

4. "Buy" one item from each of the five sections below. Spend between $65,000 and $70,000 in all.

Section	Item	Cost
1. Pets		
2. Stero		
3. Sports Equipment		
4. Motorcycles		
5. Homes for sale		

<u>Using</u> <u>Classified</u> <u>Ads</u>

Mathematics teaching objectives:

. Use the "between" place value concept.

. Apply mathematics to real world situations.

Problem-solving skills pupils <u>might</u> use:

. Use a systematic list.

. Guess and check.

Materials needed:

. One classified ad section of a local newspaper for each pair of pupils.

Comments and suggestions:

. Complete the first activity as a class. This will help pupils who have never used a classified ad section to become familiar with one.

. Pupils should be able to complete the remainder of the page with a minimum of teacher direction. Even though they are working as partners, pupils need not choose the same answers. One of the motivating elements of the activity is its personal nature. Pupils "search" the columns and ads that hold particular interest to them while completing the activity.

Answers:

Answers will vary.

PLACING CLASSIFIED ADS

> The cost for placing a classified ad depends on the number of words and how many days the ad is in the newspaper.

1. Find the section that explains the cost for placing an ad.

    How much would it cost to run this ad for one day? _____

    > USED 3-SPEED BIKE
    > Good condition.
    > Phone 222-2222 evenings

    How much would it cost to run the ad for five days? _____

    How much would it cost to run the ad for two weeks? _____

2. Use the space below. Write an ad for something you might like to sell.

    _____

    _____

    _____

    _____

    _____

    How much will it cost to run the ad for   2 days? _____

    10 days? _____   3 weeks? _____   30 days? _____

3. Suppose that one whole page of a newspaper is filled with ads like the one you wrote. About how much money would the news-paper receive to run those ads for one day? Explain your answers.

Placing Classified Ads

Mathematics teaching objectives:

. Use addition and multiplication.

. Apply mathematics to a real world situation.

Problem-solving skills pupils might use:

. Use a systematic list.

. Make predictions based upon data.

Materials needed:

. One classified ad section of a local newspaper for each pair of pupils

Comments and suggestions:

. You probably will want pupils to complete the activity, "Using Classified Ads," prior to doing this activity.

. Do no. 1 as a class. It is essential that pupils understand how classified ads are "priced" before they complete the remainder of the page.

. Pupils should be able to complete nos. 2 and 3 with a minimum of teacher direction. Although sharing the use of the classified ad section, partners need not "share" answers to the 2nd activity.

. When most pupils are finished, share answers and discuss results. Many of the pupils will want to "read" their ads, but some may choose not to do so.

Answers:

1. Answers will vary, depending upon what newspaper is used.

2-3. Answers will vary.

THE PRICE IS RIGHT

TEACHER:

Collect pictures of items of interest to your pupils from newspapers, ads, catalogs, flyers, etc. Cover up the prices of the items. (Or make transparencies of appropriate newspaper ads and black out the prices from pupil view.)

Too Low	Too High

Make this chart on the chalkboard.

Divide the class into two teams.

Hold up one of the pictures.

Have pupils from each team, in turn, guess what the price might be.

As pupils announce guesses, record the guesses in the appropriate column (Too High/Too Low).

Pupil who names correct price scores a point for own team.

The Price Is Right

Mathematics teaching objectives:

- Compare and order numbers (money values).
- Use place value concepts.

Problem-solving skills pupils <u>might</u> use:

- Guess and check.
- Make decisions based upon data.

Comments and suggestions:

- Play two or three games, keeping each table of guesses on the chalkboard. The "mystery number" should be placed above each table after it has been identified. Follow up the games with a discussion of strategies used to make good guesses. Most pupils begin by making random guesses. A useful strategy is to make "halfway" guesses until the mystery number is found.
- Some pupils may not understand why their guesses are not possible; for example, guessing $129 when $125 was already too high. Pupils could play the game in pairs with pupils who understand helping those who are confused.

Answers:

Answers will vary depending upon the mystery number.

MAKING ESTIMATES

> An estimate is a "good guess." Estimates can be used when you don't need an exact answer.

1. Your teacher will pick an article from the newspaper.

   Count the number of words in the first line of the article. _____

   Estimate the number of words in the first 5 lines of the article. _____

   Find the actual number of words in the first 5 lines of the article. _____

   How close was your estimate? _____

2. Pick an article from the front page of the newspaper.
   Copy its headline: _____

   Estimate the number of words in the entire article: _____

   Explain how you made your estimate:

3. Estimate the number of words on the entire front page: _____
   Explain your estimate:

Making Estimates

Mathematics teaching objectives:

. Use addition or multiplication skills to make reasonable estimates.

Problem-solving skills pupils <u>might</u> use:

. Make a reasonable estimate.

. Make predictions based upon data.

Materials needed:

. One newspaper for each pair of pupils

Comments and suggestions:

. Complete the first activity as a class. Have pupils complete the remainder of the lesson on their own, working in pairs.

. When most pupils have completed the lesson, discuss the second activity. Most likely, several pairs of pupils will have selected the same articles, so results can be compared.

. Finish the lesson with a discussion of the third activity. Determine the range of answers. Pupils with particularly high or low estimates might be asked to justify their responses.

Answers:

Answers will vary.

WHAT DID I BUY?

$39.79

$9.99

$99

$68.89

19.29

$4.98

#$15	#$70	#$420	#$280	#$300
#$400	#$210	#$160	#$35	#$80
#$240	#$90	#$350	#$120	#$50
#$20	#$140	#$200	#$100	#$360
#$500	#$1000	#$45	#$40	#$25

What <u>Did</u> <u>I</u> <u>Buy?</u>

Mathematics teaching objectives:

. Practice with rounding skills and mental arithmetic.

Problem-solving skills pupils <u>might</u> use:

. Make a reasonable estimate.

. Guess and check.

Materials needed:

. One acetate transparency of the activity page

. Overhead projector

. Grease pencil, crayon, or AV pen or pencil

Comments and suggestions:

. Display a transparency of the activity, using an overhead projector.

. Call pupils' attention to the store items. Ask:

"Which item costs about $20?" (watch)

"Which item costs about $5? " (ring)

"About how much does the camera cost?" ($70)

"I bought two items and spent about $45. Which two items did I buy?"
(radio and ring)

"I bought <u>three</u> items and spent about $100. Which three items did I buy?"
(camera, watch, and tennis racket <u>or</u> two radios and one watch)

. Explain that the class is going to play a tic-tac-toe game using the store items and the displayed game board.

. Play one side of the room against the other side (X's and O's).

. Take turns calling on pupils from each side.

. The pupil who is selected picks any square and names two or three store items that would cost "about" the amount named in the square.

. If the pupil is correct, the teacher marks that square with either an X or O.

. The winner is the first side of the room to get <u>three</u> of its marks in a row, column, or diagonal.

Extension:

The grease pencil or crayon will wipe off the acetate easily, so the game can be reused a number of times. The game loses its value once pupils are proficient at "rounding" and have developed some winning strategies for placing their X's and O's.

> Everyone needs to learn math. Our daily lives require that we add, subtract, multiply, and divide.

1. Look through a newspaper. Find one article about each of these basic human needs: food, clothing, shelter, and transportation.

   Cut out the articles. Circle the numbers used in each of the articles.

2. Make up an addition problem about one of the articles.
   Do a subtraction problem for a different article.
   Do a multiplication problem for a third article.
   Do a division problem for the fourth article.

Story Problem	Solution
Addition:	
Subtraction:	
Multiplication:	
Division:	

Math In Our Daily Lives

Mathematics teaching objectives:

. Apply the whole number operations of addition, subtraction, multiplication, and division to real world situations.

Problem-solving skills pupils might use:

. Creates own problems based upon data.

Materials needed:

. One newspaper for each pair of pupils

Comments and suggestions:

. Spend a few minutes discussing why food, clothing, shelter, and transportation are considered to be "basic human needs." Then allow pupils about 10 minutes to find articles in their newspaper about these basic needs and circle the numbers used in the articles.

. After pupils have located articles, ask for a suggestion of an "addition story problem" about one of the articles. If time allows, let several different pupils suggest addition story problems. Pupils may need help in "wording" the problems. It helps to remind them that a story problem gives certain facts and asks a question.

. After discussing possible addition story problems, have pupils complete the activity on their own or with a partner.

. When most pupils have completed the lesson, provide some time for pupils who wish to do so to share the stories they wrote.

Answers:

Answers will vary.

DIGIT MULTIPLICATION – A

Follow the directions your teacher gives.

Game 1

☐ ☐
X ☐

Target Product: _112_

My Product: _____

Score: _____

Game 2

☐ ☐
X ☐

Target Product: _189_

My Product: _____

Score: _____

Game 3

☐ ☐
X ☐

Target Product: _350_

My Product: _____

Score: _____

Game 4

☐ ☐
X ☐

Target Product: _499_

My Product: _____

Score: _____

Game 5

☐ ☐
X ☐

Target Product: _600_

My Product: _____

Score: _____

Digit Multiplication - A

Mathematics teaching objectives:

. Practice multiplication with 1-digit multipliers.

. Use place value concepts.

Problem-solving skills pupils might use:

. Guess and check.

. Look for a pattern.

Materials needed:

. One set of ten small cards numbered 0 to 9. See page 2   for a master.

Comments and suggestions:

. This is a whole class game-type activity. Space is provided on the worksheet for five games. For each game,

  1. call pupils' attention to the target number for that game.

  2. announce that the winner of the game is the person to create a problem
      whose answer is closest to the target without going over.

  3. mix deck of ten cards well. Draw out one card at a time.

  4. as cards are drawn, announce the digit on each aloud. Pupils write
      the digits, as they are announced, in spaces of their own choosing.

  5. when all spaces are filled, pupils solve the problem they have
      created. The answer to that problem (if lower than target number)
      is subtracted from the target number to determine the pupil's score.

      If the answer is more than the target answer, the pupil gets an
      automatic score of 50.

  The winner is the player whose score for all the games is lowest.

. Rather than find a score for all five games, each can be played separately
  with a score of zero given for answers more than the target answer.

Answers:

    Answers will vary.

DIGIT MULTIPLICATION – B

Follow the directions your teacher gives.

Game 1 ☐ ☐ ☐
☐
X _____

Target Product: _1,120_

My Product: _____

Score: _____

Game 2 ☐ ☐ ☐
☐
X _____

Target Product: _2,003_

My Product: _____

Score: _____

Game 3 ☐ ☐ ☐
☐
X _____

Target Product: _3,892_

My Product: _____

Score: _____

Game 4 ☐ ☐ ☐
☐
X _____

Target Product: _5,009_

My Product: _____

Score: _____

Game 5 ☐ ☐ ☐
☐
X _____

Target Product: _6,000_

My Product: _____

Score: _____

<u>Digit</u> <u>Multiplication</u> - <u>B</u>

Mathematics teaching objectives:

. Practice multiplication with 1-digit multipliers.

. Use place value concepts.

Problem-solving skills pupils <u>might</u> use:

. Guess and check.

. Look for a pattern.

Materials needed:

. One set of ten small cards numbered 0 to 9. See page 2 for a master.

Comments and suggestions:

. This is a whole class game-type activity. Space is provided on the worksheet for five games. For each game,

   1. call pupils' attention to the target number for that game.

   2. announce that the winner of the game is the person to create a
       problem whose answer is closest to the target <u>without</u> <u>going</u> <u>over</u>.

   3. mix deck of ten cards well. Draw out <u>one</u> <u>card</u> <u>at</u> <u>a</u> <u>time</u>.

   4. as cards are drawn, announce the digit on each aloud. Pupils write
       the digits, <u>as</u> <u>they</u> <u>are</u> <u>announced</u>, in spaces of their own choosing.

   5. when all spaces are filled, pupils solve the problem they have
       created. The answer to that problem (if lower than target number)
       is subtracted from the target number to determine pupil's score.

       If the answer is more than the target answer, the pupil gets an
       automatic score of 200.

   The winner is the player whose score for all the games is lowest.

. Rather than find a score for all five games, each can be played separately
   with a score of zero given for answers more than the target answer.

Answers:

   Answers will vary.

DIGIT MULTIPLICATION - C

Follow the directions your teacher gives.

Game 1

☐ ☐ ☐ ☐
☐
X _____

Target Product: _10,000_

My Product: _____

Score: _____

Game 2

☐ ☐ ☐ ☐
X ☐
_____

Target Product: _20,000_

My Product: _____

Score: _____

Game 3

☐ ☐ ☐ ☐
X ☐
_____

Target Product: _39,000_

My Product: _____

Score: _____

Game 4

☐ ☐ ☐ ☐
X ☐
_____

Target Product: _51,000_

My Product: _____

Score: _____

Game 5

☐ ☐ ☐ ☐
☐
X _____

Target Product: _60,000_

My Product: _____

Score: _____

PSM 82

<u>Digit</u> <u>Multiplication</u> - <u>C</u>

Mathematics teaching objectives:

. Practice multiplication with 1-digit multipliers.

. Use place value concepts

Problem-solving skills pupils <u>might</u> use:

. Guess and check.

. Look for a pattern.

Materials needed:

. One set of ten small cards numbered 0 to 9. See page 2   for a master.

Comments and suggestions:

. This is a whole class game-type activity. Space is provided on the worksheet for five games. For each game,

1. call pupils' attention to the target number for that game.

2. announce that the winner of the game is the person to create a
problem whose answer is closest to the target <u>without</u> <u>going</u> <u>over</u>.

3. mix deck of ten cards well. Draw out <u>one</u> <u>card</u> <u>at</u> <u>a</u> <u>time</u>.

4. as cards are drawn, announce the digit on each aloud. Pupils write
the digits, <u>as</u> <u>they</u> <u>are</u> <u>announced</u>, in spaces of their own choosing.

5. when all spaces are filled, pupils solve the problem they have
created. The answer to that problem (if lower than target number)
is subtracted from the target number to determine pupil's score.

If the answer is more than the target answer, the pupil gets an
automatic score of 500.

The winner is the player whose score for all the games is lowest.

. Rather than find a score for all five games, each can be played separately
with a score of zero given for answers more than the target answer.

Answers:

Answers will vary.

DIGIT MULTIPLICATION - D

Follow the directions your teacher gives.

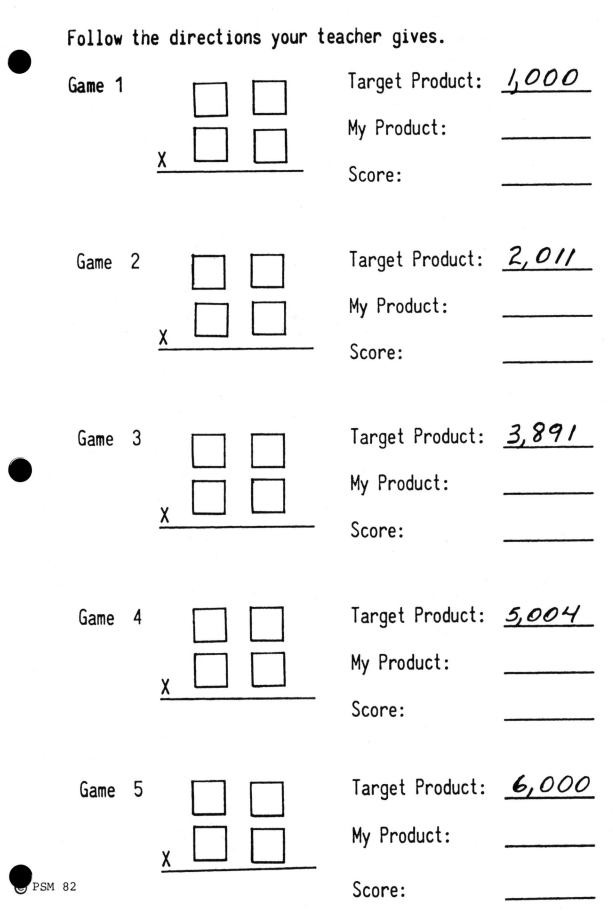

Game 1   □ □
        X □ □

Target Product: _1,000_

My Product: _____

Score: _____

Game 2   □ □
        X □ □

Target Product: _2,011_

My Product: _____

Score: _____

Game 3   □ □
        X □ □

Target Product: _3,891_

My Product: _____

Score: _____

Game 4   □ □
        X □ □

Target Product: _5,004_

My Product: _____

Score: _____

Game 5   □ □
        X □ □

Target Product: _6,000_

My Product: _____

Score: _____

Digit Multiplication - D

Mathematics teaching objectives:

. Practice 2-digit multiplication.

. Use place value concepts.

Problem-solving skills pupils might use:

. Guess and check.

. Look for a pattern.

Materials needed:

. One set of ten small cards numbered 0 to 9. See page 2   for a master.

Comments and suggestions:

. This is a whole class game-type activity. Space is provided on the worksheet for five games.

    1. call pupils' attention to the target number for that game.

    2. announce that the winner of the game is the person to create a
   problem whose answer is closest to the target <u>without</u> <u>going</u> <u>over</u>.

    3. mix deck of ten cards well. Draw out <u>one</u> <u>card</u> <u>at</u> <u>a</u> <u>time</u>.

    4. as cards are drawn, announce the digit on each aloud. Pupils write
   the digits, <u>as</u> <u>they</u> <u>are</u> <u>announced</u>, in spaces of their own choosing.

    5. when all spaces are filled, pupils solve the problem they have
   created. The answer to that problem (if lower than target number)
   is subtracted from the target number to determine pupil's score.

        If the answer is more than the target answer, the pupil gets an
   automatic score of 250.

The winner is the player whose score for all the games is lowest.

. Rather than find a score for all **five** games, each can be played separately
   with a score of zero given for answers more than the target answer.

Answers:

Answers will vary.

MULTIPLICATION TRIANGLE PUZZLES - A

1. Here are some 2-story triangle puzzles.

   Finish these 2-story triangle puzzles.

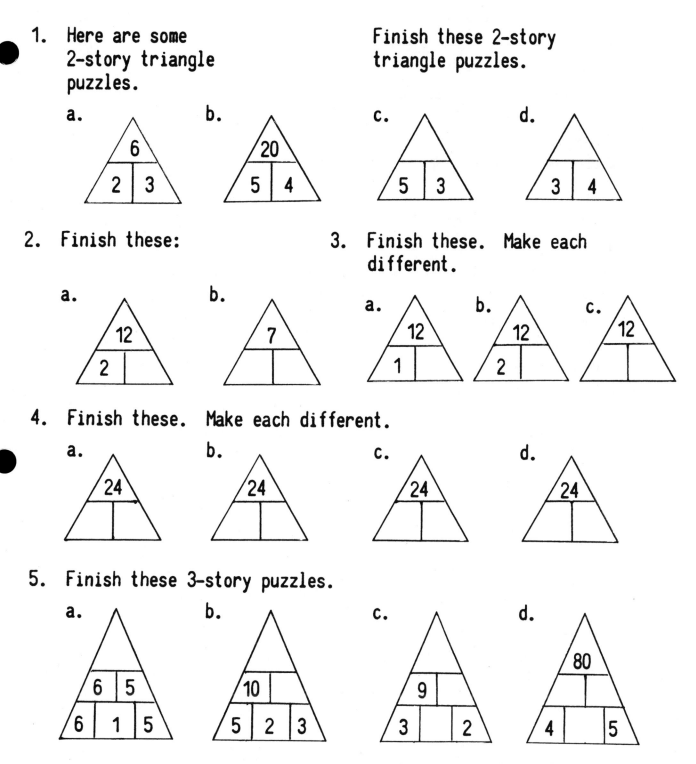

   a.   b.   c.   d.

2. Finish these:

   a.   b.

3. Finish these. Make each different.

   a.   b.   c.

4. Finish these. Make each different.

   a.   b.   c.   d.

5. Finish these 3-story puzzles.

   a.   b.   c.   d.

EXTENSION

Use the back of this page. Make up some 3-story puzzles for your classmates to solve.

Multiplication Triangle Puzzles - A

Mathematics teaching objectives:

. Practice using basic multiplication facts.

. Use mental arithmetic.

Problem-solving skills pupils might use:

. Guess and check.

. Work backwards.

. Eliminate possibilities.

Materials needed:

. None

Comments and suggestions:

. Work several problems together as a class. Be certain pupils understand how the "upper floor" numbers are determined. Then have pupils complete the remaining problems on their own.

. Problem 5d requires pupils to "guess and check" and then "work backwards." Encourage pupils to persist until they find a solution that works.

Answers:

1. e. 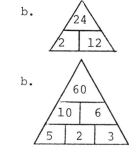   d.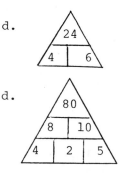

2. a.   b.

3. Accept these 3 answers, in any order.

   a.    b.   c.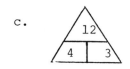

4. Accept these 4 answers, in any order.

   a.   b.   c.   d.

5. a.   b. 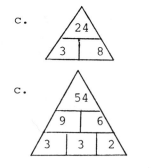   c.   d.

TIC TAC TOE

1. This game needs two players.
2. Pick a number from column 1 and a number from column 2.
3. Multiply the numbers on your calculator. Find the answer and mark it with an X or O.
4. Play like regular Tic Tac Toe and try to get three in a row.

1	2
11	41
21	51
31	61

1	2
19	39
33	27
25	45

1	2
41	6
16	26
61	36

1891	671	1581
561	1271	1071
1281	861	451

Game A

513	1485	741
855	1125	1287
9975	675	891

Game B

96	416	366
576	1476	2196
1586	246	1066

Game C

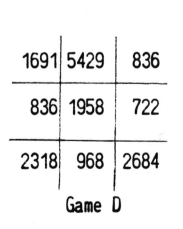

1	2
22	44
19	38
61	89

1691	5429	836
836	1958	722
2318	968	2684

Game D

5. Create your own Tic Tac Toe.

1	2

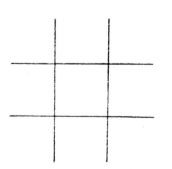

Tic Tac Toe

Mathematics teaching objectives:

. Use place value concepts to make reasonable estimates.

Problem-solving skills pupils _might_ use:

. Guess and check.

. Make reasonable estimates.

. Record solution attempts.

Materials needed:

. Calculator

Comments and suggestions:

. Discuss the general directions. Play Game A as a class by having one side of the room compete against the other side of the room. Then have pupils form pairs and play the remaining games.

. Recording solution attempts is important to avoid choosing a spot that already has been taken. The attempts may also help in making reasonable guesses later in the game.

Answers:

This activity has no answers. The use of the calculator makes it self-checking.

DIGIT DIVISION - A

Follow the directions your teacher gives.

Game 1

$\square \overline{)\square\ \square\ \square}$

Target Quotient: 50

My Quotient: _____

Score: _____

Game 2

$\square \overline{)\square\ \square\ \square}$

Target Quotient: 100

My Quotient: _____

Score: _____

Game 3

$\square \overline{)\square\ \square\ \square}$

Target Quotient: 200

My Quotient: _____

Score: _____

Game 4

$\square \overline{)\square\ \square\ \square}$

Target Quotient: 300

My Quotient: _____

Score: _____

Game 5

$\square \overline{)\square\ \square\ \square}$

Target Quotient: 400

My Quotient: _____

Score: _____

<u>Digit Division</u> - <u>A</u>

Mathematics teaching objectives:

- Practice long division using 1-digit divisors.
- Use place value concepts.

Problem-solving skills pupils might use:

- Guess and check.
- Look for a pattern.

Materials needed:

- One set of ten small cards numbered 0 to 9. See page 2   for a master.

Comments and suggestions:

- This is a whole class game-type activity. Space is provided on the work-sheet for five games. For each game,

    1. call pupils' attention to the target number for that game.

    2. announce that the winner of the game is the person to create a problem whose answer is closest to the target <u>without</u> <u>going</u> <u>over</u>.

    3. mix deck of ten cards well. Draw out <u>one</u> <u>card</u> <u>at</u> <u>a</u> <u>time</u>.

    4. as cards are drawn, announce the digit on each aloud. Pupils write the digits, <u>as</u> <u>they</u> <u>are</u> <u>announced</u>, in spaces of their own choosing.

    5. when all spaces are filled, pupils solve the problem they have created. The answer to that problem (if lower than target number) is subtracted from the target number to determine pupil's score. Drop (or ignore) any remainders when determining the score.

        If the answer is more than the target answer, the pupil gets an automatic score of 50.

    The winner is the player whose score for all the games is lowest.

- Rather than find a score for all **five** games, each can be played separately with a score of zero given for answers more than the target answer.

Answers:

   Answers will vary.

DIGIT DIVISION - B

Follow the directions your teacher gives.

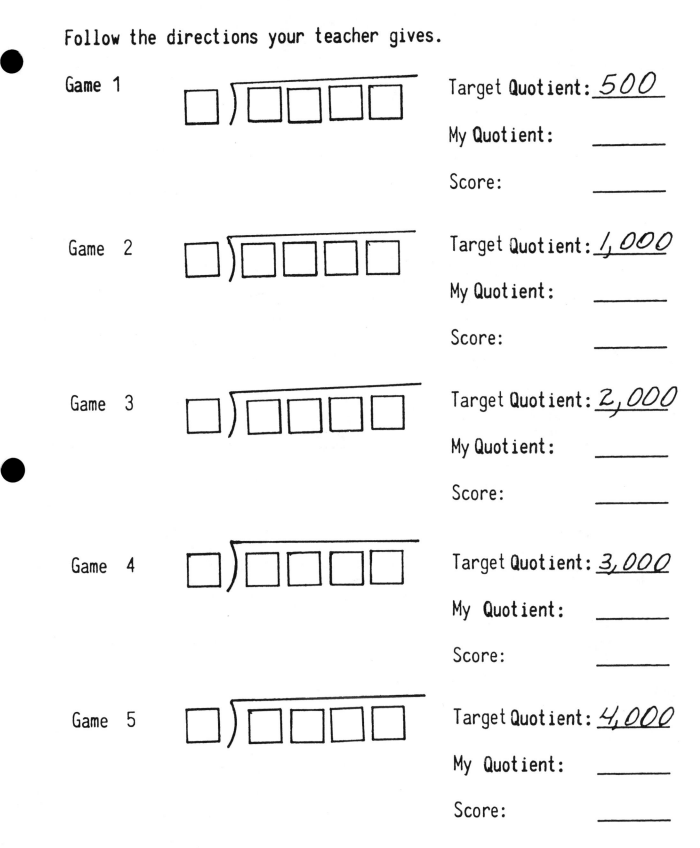

Game 1   ☐ ⟌ ☐ ☐ ☐ ☐   Target Quotient: _500_

My Quotient: _____

Score: _____

Game 2   ☐ ⟌ ☐ ☐ ☐ ☐   Target Quotient: _1,000_

My Quotient: _____

Score: _____

Game 3   ☐ ⟌ ☐ ☐ ☐ ☐   Target Quotient: _2,000_

My Quotient: _____

Score: _____

Game 4   ☐ ⟌ ☐ ☐ ☐ ☐   Target Quotient: _3,000_

My Quotient: _____

Score: _____

Game 5   ☐ ⟌ ☐ ☐ ☐ ☐   Target Quotient: _4,000_

My Quotient: _____

Score: _____

<u>Digit Division</u> - <u>B</u>

Mathematics teaching objectives:

 . Practice long division using 1-digit divisors.

 . Use place value concepts.

Problem-solving skills pupils <u>might</u> use:

 . Guess and check.

 . Look for a pattern.

Materials needed:

 . One set of ten small cards numbered 0 to 9. See page 2   for a master.

Comments and suggestions:

 . This is a whole class game-type activity. Space is provided on the worksheet for five games. For each game,

   1. call pupils' attention to the target number for that game.

   2. announce that the winner of the game is the person to create a problem
       whose answer is closest to the target <u>without</u> <u>going</u> <u>over</u>.

   3. mix deck of ten cards well. Draw out <u>one</u> <u>card</u> <u>at</u> <u>a</u> <u>time</u>.

   4. as cards are drawn, announce the digit on each aloud. Pupils write
       the digits, <u>as</u> <u>they</u> <u>are</u> <u>announced</u>, in spaces of their own choosing.

   5. when all spaces are filled, pupils solve the problem they have
       created. The answer to that problem (if lower than target number) is
       subtracted from the target number to determine pupil's score. Drop
       (or ignore) any remainders when determining the score.

       If the answer is more than the target answer , the pupil gets an
       automatic score of 200.

   The winner is the player whose score for all the games is lowest.

 . Rather than find a score for all five games, each can be played separately
   with a score of zero given for answers more than the target answer.

   Answers:

   Answers will vary.

DIGIT DIVISION - C

Follow the directions your teacher gives.

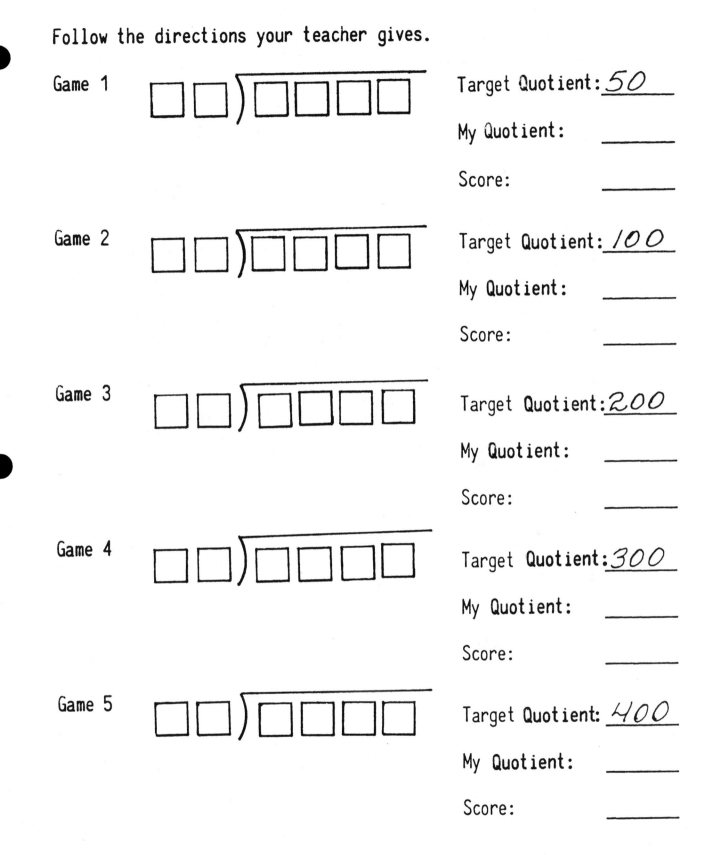

Game 1 ⬜⬜)⬜⬜⬜⬜

Target Quotient: 50

My Quotient: _____

Score: _____

Game 2 ⬜⬜)⬜⬜⬜⬜

Target Quotient: 100

My Quotient: _____

Score: _____

Game 3 ⬜⬜)⬜⬜⬜⬜

Target Quotient: 200

My Quotient: _____

Score: _____

Game 4 ⬜⬜)⬜⬜⬜⬜

Target Quotient: 300

My Quotient: _____

Score: _____

Game 5 ⬜⬜)⬜⬜⬜⬜

Target Quotient: 400

My Quotient: _____

Score: _____

Digit Division - C

Mathematics teaching objectives:

. Practice long division using 2-digit divisors.

. Use place value concepts.

Problem-solving skills pupils might use:

. Guess and check.

. Look for a pattern.

Materials needed:

. One set of ten small cards numbered 0-9. See page 2   for a master.

Comments and suggestions:

. This is a whole class, game-type activity. Space is provided to play
  5 games. For each game,

    1. call pupils' attention to the target number for that game.

    2. announce that the winner of the game is the person to create a problem
        whose answer is closest to the target without going over.

    3. mix deck of ten cards well. Draw out one card at a time.

    4. as cards are drawn, announce the digit on each aloud. Pupils write
        the digits, as they are announced, in spaces of their own choosing.

    5. when all spaces are filled, pupils solve the problem they have
        created. The answer to that problem (if lower than target number) is
        subtracted from the target number to determine pupil's score. Drop
        (or ignore) any remainders when determining the score.

        If the answer is more than the target answer, the pupil gets an
        automatic score of 250.

        The winner is the player whose score for all the games is lowest.

. Rather than find a score for all five games, each can be played separately
  with a score of zero given for answers more than the target answer.

Answers:

Answers will vary.

FIND THE FACTORS - A

Follow the directions your teacher gives.

Factors: 11   32   49   73   92
                19   41   58   81

Gameboard:

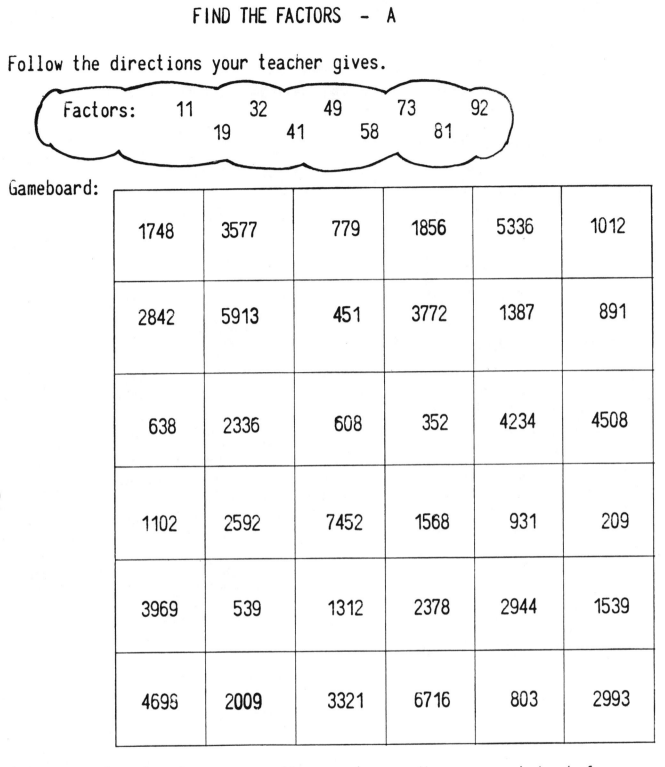

1748	3577	779	1856	5336	1012
2842	5913	451	3772	1387	891
638	2336	608	352	4234	4508
1102	2592	7452	1568	931	209
3969	539	1312	2378	2944	1539
4699	2009	3321	6716	803	2993

Play this tic-tac-toe game with a partner. Use one worksheet for the two of you.

Take turns. Pick two numbers from the factors section. Multiply the numbers. Place your mark (X or O) in the space with that answer.

Winner is the first player to get <u>four</u> marks in a row, column, or diagonal.

-103-

<u>Find</u> <u>The</u> <u>Factors</u> - <u>A</u>

Mathematics teaching objectives:

- Practice multiplying 2-digit numbers.
- Practice approximating answers to 2-digit multiplication problems.
- Practice using rounding skills.

Problem-solving skills pupils <u>might</u> use:

- Guess and check.
- Make a reasonable estimate.
- Look for a pattern.
- Use previously-acquired knowledge.

Materials needed:

- Extra copies of worksheet
- Calculators (optional)

Comments and suggestions:

- Discuss directions. Have pupils pair up and play the game.
- Have extra copies on hand for pupils who finish ahead of others and wish to play a second game.
- Use of differently colored markers eases the need for extra copies.
- For a quicker game, play for <u>three</u>, instead of four, marks in a row.
- Using calculators allows pupils to really concentrate on estimation skills and allows the activity to move along quickly.
- If pupils do not seem to be estimating products before selecting factors, take time to review rounding skills and techniques for approximating answers.
- This activity can be completed as a whole class game with one side of the room competing against the other side. If you wish to use the activity in this manner, make a transparent copy of the worksheet and display it with an overhead projector. Playing the game as a whole class activity will give you more opportunities to discuss use of rounding and approximation skills.

FIND THE FACTORS - B

Follow the directions your teacher gives:

Factors: 110   301   497   706   987
            21   39   62   79

Gameboard:

819	18,662	1,302	696,822	77,660	1,659
77,973	6,321	38,493	4,290	43,772	55,774
8,690	20,727	350,882	2,310	61,194	108,570
490,539	14,826	33,110	27,534	6,820	39,263
212,506	30,814	11,739	10,437	54,670	3,081
19,383	2,418	149,597	4,898	23,779	297,087

Play this tic-tac-toe game with a partner. Use one worksheet for the two of you.

Take turns. Pick two numbers from the factors section. Multiply the numbers. Place your mark (X or 0) in the space with that answer.

Winner is the first player to get <u>four</u> marks in a row, column, or diagonal.

Find The Factors - B

Mathematics teaching objectives:

- Practice multiplying 2- and 3-digit numbers.

- Practice approximating answers to multiplication problems.

- Practice using rounding skills.

Problem-solving skills pupils might use:

- Guess and check.

- Make a reasonable estimate.

- Look for a pattern.

- Use previously-acquired knowledge.

Materials needed:

- Extra copies of worksheet

- Calculators (optional)

Comments and suggestions:

- Discuss directions. Have pupils pair up and play the game.

- Have extra copies on hand for pupils who finish ahead of others and wish to play a second game.

- Use of differently colored markers eases the need for extra copies.

- For a quicker game, play for three, instead of four, marks in a row.

- Using calculators allows pupils to really concentrate on estimation skills and allows the activity to move along quickly.

- If pupils do not seem to be estimating products before selecting factors, take time to review rounding skills and techniques for approximating answers.

- This activity can be completed as a whole class game with one side of the room competing against the other side. If you wish to use the activity in this manner, make a transparent copy of the worksheet and display it with an overhead projector. Playing the game as a whole class activity will give you more opportunities to discuss use of rounding and approximation skills.

FIND THE FACTORS - C

Follow the directions your teacher gives.

Factors: 106   312   493   716   920
         203   405   585   811

Gameboard:

85,966	82,215	186,760	289,980	118,755	75,896
474,435	145,348	153,816	372,600	100,079	418,860
352,988	746,120	33,072	253,032	538,200	199,665
288,405	580,676	62,010	164,633	52,258	223,392
97,520	399,823	287,040	453,560	63,336	182,520
658,720	328,455	21,518	236,925	126,360	42,930

Play this tic-tac-toe game with a partner. Use one worksheet for the two of you.

Take turns. Pick two numbers from the factors section. Multiply the numbers. Place your mark (X or 0) in the space with that answer.

Winner is the first player to get <u>four</u> marks in a row, column, or diagonal.

<u>Find</u> <u>The</u> <u>Factors</u> - <u>C</u>

Mathematics teaching objectives:

- Practice multiplying two 3-digit numbers.
- Practice approximating answers to multiplication problems.
- Practice using rounding skills.

Problem-solving skills pupils <u>might</u> use:

- Guess and check.
- Make a reasonable estimate.
- Look for a pattern.
- Use previously-acquired knowledge.

Materials needed:

- Extra copies of worksheet
- Calculators (optional)

Comments and suggestions:

- Discuss directions. Have pupils pair up and play the game.
- Have extra copies on hand for pupils who finish ahead of others and wish to play a second game.
- Use of differently colored markers eases the need for extra copies.
- For a quicker game, play for <u>three</u>, instead of four, marks in a row.
- Using calculators allows pupils to really concentrate on estimation skills and allows the activity to move along quickly.
- If pupils do not seem to be estimating products before selecting factors, take time to review rounding skills and techniques for approximating answers.
- This activity can be completed as a whole class game with one side of the room competing against the other side. If you wish to use the activity in this manner, make a transparent copy of the worksheet and display it with an overhead projector. Playing the game as a whole class activity will give you more opportunities to discuss use of rounding and approoximation skills.

FIND THE FACTORS - DECIMALS

FACTORS:	2.3 4.6 5.9 3.8 3.4 1.9 2.9 5.2 4.7				
17.68	5.51	10.81	30.68	22.42	15.08
10.58	11.21	13.63	27.14	8.74	27.73
19.76	13.57	8.74	11.02	20.06	12.92
23.92	6.46	6.67	7.22	15.64	4.37
7.82	17.86	9.88	9.86	8.93	17.48
17.11	21.62	13.34	15.98	11.96	24.44

Play this tic-tac-toe game with a partner. Use one worksheet for the two of you.

Take turns. Pick two numbers from the Factors section. Multiply the numbers. Place your mark (X or 0) in the space with that answer.

Winner is the first player to get four marks in a row, column, or diagonal.

© PSM 82

Find the Factors - Decimals

Mathematics teaching objectives:

- Practice multiplying two decimals.
- Practice approximating answers to decimal multiplication problems.
- Practice using rounding skills.

Problem-solving skills pupils **might** use:

- Guess and check.
- Look for a pattern.
- Use previously-acquired knowledge.
- Make a reasonable estimate.

Materials needed:

- Extra copies of worksheet
- Calculators (optional)

Comments and suggestions:

- Discuss directions. Have pupils pair up and play the game.
- Have extra copies on hand for pupils who finish ahead of others and wish to play a second game.
- Use of differently colored markers eases the need for extra copies.
- For a quicker game, play for **three**, instead of four, marks in a row.
- Using calculators allows pupils to really concentrate on estimation skills and allows the activity to move along quickly.
- If pupils do not seem to be estimating products before selecting factors, take time to review rounding skills and techniques for approximating answers.
- This activity can be completed as a whole class game with one side of the room competing against the other side. If you wish to use the activity in this manner, make a transparent copy of the worksheet and display it with an overhead projector. Playing the game as a whole class activity will give you more opportunities to discuss use of rounding and approximation skills.

II. STORY PROBLEMS

FACTS AND QUESTIONS

A word problem gives some facts and asks a question.

1. The facts you need to solve the problem below are underlined. Draw a loop around the question the problem asks.

Lee has 15 toy cars. Jan has 24 toy cars. How many cars do they have in all?

2. In each problem below   . underline the facts.
                                   . loop the question.

a. Sue had $15. She spent $9.
How much money does she have left?

b. How many animals does Bob have?
He has 13 cats, 2 dogs, and 15 rabbits.

c. Todd gave Jim six candy bars. Jim ate two of them.
How many candy bars does Jim have now?

d. Is Mike older than Bill? Mike is 23 years old. Bill is 32 years old.

e. Carlos has 23 red pens, 18 blue pens, and 15 black pens.
How many pens does he have?

f. Lou has 17 dollars. She needs 20 dollars to buy a new pair of boots. How much more money does she need?

g. Susan has 13 balloons. Carl gave her 3 more.
How many balloons does she have now?

h. Last week Bill watched six cartoon shows, three quiz shows, and twelve mysteries.
How many T.V. shows did he watch?

i. Lee sold 35 tickets to the school carnival. Chris sold 53 tickets. How many more tickets did Chris sell than Lee?

Facts And Questions

Mathematics teaching objectives:

. Recognize some properties of word problems.

Problem-solving skills pupils <u>might</u> use:

. Look for a pattern.

Materials needed:

. None

Comments and suggestions:

. Discuss part 1 as a class. Do the first few examples in part 2 together.

. Have pupils complete the activity on their own.

. Discuss results. Ask pupils if they notice any patterns in the answers.

Answers:

2. a. Sue had $15. She spent $9. How much money does she have left?

   b. How many animals does Bob have? He has 13 cats, 2 dogs, and 15 rabbits.

   c. Todd gave Jim six candy bars. Jim ate two of them. How many candy bars does Jim have now?

   d. Is Mike older than Bill? Mike is 23 years old. Bill is 32 years old.

   e. Carlos has 23 red pens, 18 blue pens, and 15 black pens. How many pens does he have?

   f. Lou has 17 dollars. She needs 20 dollars to buy a new pair of boots. How much more money does she need?

   g. Susan has 13 balloons. Carl gave her 3 more. How many balloons does she have now?

   h. Last week Bill watched six cartoon shows, three quiz shows, and twelve mysteries. How many T.V. shows did he watch?

   i. Lee sold 35 tickets to the school carnival. Chris sold 53 tickets. How many more tickets did Chris sell than Lee?

USING NUMBER PROBLEMS TO SOLVE STORY PROBLEMS

> A word problem gives some facts and asks a question.
> Sometimes a number sentence or an arithmetic problem can
> be used to answer the question or solve the problem.

1. Tom read this story in his math book:

   | Tom read 42 books in class at school and 16 books at home. How many books in all did he read? |

   He wrote this problem to answer the question in the story.

   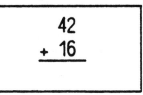

   Answer Tom's problem.

2. Write a problem to answer the question in each story below. Solve each problem.

STORY	PROBLEM
a. Lou made 35 bologna sandwiches and 12 peanut butter and jelly sandwiches. How many sandwiches did Lou make?	
b. Mike bought 36 tomato plants, 16 pepper plants and 13 straw- berry plants. How many plants did Mike buy?	
c. Mary and Jane have 68 marbles. Twenty of them are Mary's. How many belong to Jane?	

Using Number Problems To Solve Story Problems

Mathematics teaching objectives:

  . Recognize some properties of word problems.

  . Use addition and subtraction algorithms to solve word problems.

  . Compute with money amounts.

Problem-solving skills pupils might use:

  . Look for a pattern.

  . Use math symbols to translate and solve a problem.

Materials needed:

  . None

Comments and suggestions:

  . Read the story problem "boxed in" in part 1 to the class. Have pupils find the facts in the problem and the question it asks. Ask, "What number problem would we use to find the answer to the question the problem asks?" (42 + 16 = ?) Solve the problem together. (58 books)

  . Do one or two of the problems in part 2 in a similar manner. Remind pupils to label answers. Then have pupils complete the activity on their own.

  . When most pupils are finished, discuss and compare answers. Note the patterns the pupils notice.

  . If any pupils have done the Extra activity, ask them to share their stories for the class to solve.

Answers:

  1. 58 books

  2. a. $\begin{array}{r} 35 \\ +\ 12 \\ \hline 47 \end{array}$ sandwiches

  b. $\begin{array}{r} 36 \\ 16 \\ +\ 13 \\ \hline 65 \end{array}$ plants

  c. $\begin{array}{r} 68 \\ -\ 20 \\ \hline 48 \end{array}$ marbles

  d. $\begin{array}{r} 48 \\ -\ 42 \\ \hline 6 \end{array}$ words

  e. $\begin{array}{r} 16 \\ 11 \\ +\ 42 \\ \hline 69 \end{array}$ kilometers

  f. $\begin{array}{r} \$20 \\ -\ 12 \\ \hline \$\ 8 \end{array}$

  g. $\begin{array}{r} 31 \\ -\ 9 \\ \hline 22 \end{array}$ years

  h. $\begin{array}{r} 85 \\ -\ 24 \\ \hline 61 \end{array}$ pages

  Extra: Answers will vary.

Using Number Problems To Solve Story Problems (cont.)

STORY	PROBLEM
d. There were 48 words on the spelling test. Bess got 42 words right. How many words did she miss?	
e. Alice rode her bike 16 kilometers on Monday, 11 kilometers on Tuesday, and 42 kilometers on Wednesday. How many kilometers in all did she ride?	
f. Bill paid 12 dollars for a shirt. He gave the clerk a $20 bill. How much change did he get back?	
g. Beth is 31 years old. Her brother is 9 years younger. How old is her brother?	
h. Joy began reading her book on page 24 and read to page 85. How many pages did she read?	

Extra: Make up some stories of your own. Write the number problems used to solve the questions in your stories. Solve the problems.

HIDDEN NUMBERS

A word problem gives some facts and asks a question. Some of the number facts may be "hidden" as words. To finish these problems you must first change the hidden fact from a word to a number.

Read and discuss this problem: ⟶ Jim has 8 pairs of shoes. He polished each shoe. How many shoes did he polish?

. What is the hidden number word?
. What is the answer to the problem?

Find and loop the hidden number word (or words) in the problems below. Solve each problem. Label your answers.

PROBLEMS	WORKSPACE
1. Mindy had a dozen cupcakes. She gave 5 of them away. How many cupcakes did she have left?	
2. Betty has a quarter. Joe has 30¢. How much more money does Joe have than Betty?	
3. Lem drinks 3 glasses of milk a day. How many glasses of milk does he drink in a week?	

Hidden Numbers

Mathematics teaching objectives:

- Solve word problems containing "hidden number" words such as <u>pair</u>, <u>dozen</u>, and <u>half-dollar</u>.
- Compute with money amounts.

Problem-solving skills pupils <u>might</u> use:

- Look for a pattern.
- Use math symbols to translate and solve a problem.

Materials needed:

- None

Comments and suggestions:

- Read the word problem in the "cloud" to the class. Ask class to identify the "hidden" number word in the problem. (Reread aloud if needed.) Solve the problem together.
- Ask pupils to identify any "hidden" number words in the remaining word problems and to "loop" them before solving the problems. Remind pupils to label answers.
- When most pupils have completed the assignment, discuss answers. If any pupils have completed the Extra activity, ask them to share the word problems they wrote.

Answers:

1. dozen

$$
\begin{array}{r}
12 \\
-\ 5 \\
\hline
7 \text{ cupcakes}
\end{array}
$$

2. quarter

$$
\begin{array}{r}
30¢ \\
-\ 25¢ \\
\hline
5¢
\end{array}
\quad \text{or} \quad
\begin{array}{r}
\$.30 \\
-\ .25 \\
\hline
\$.05
\end{array}
$$

3. week

$$
\begin{array}{r}
3 \\
\times\ 7 \\
\hline
21 \text{ glasses}
\end{array}
\quad \text{or} \quad
\begin{array}{r}
7 \\
\times\ 3 \\
\hline
21 \text{ glasses}
\end{array}
\quad \text{or} \quad
\begin{array}{r}
3 \\
3 \\
3 \\
3 \\
3 \\
+\ 3 \\
\hline
21 \text{ glasses}
\end{array}
$$

4. quarter
   dime

$$
\begin{array}{r}
25¢ \\
+\ 10¢ \\
\hline
35¢
\end{array}
\quad \text{or} \quad
\begin{array}{r}
\$.25 \\
+\ .10 \\
\hline
\$.35
\end{array}
$$

5. half-dollar

$$
\begin{array}{r}
79¢ \\
-\ 50¢ \\
\hline
29¢
\end{array}
\quad \text{or} \quad
\begin{array}{r}
\$.79 \\
-\ .50 \\
\hline
\$.29
\end{array}
$$

6. half hour

$$
\begin{array}{r}
30 \\
+\ 20 \\
\hline
50 \text{ minutes}
\end{array}
$$

<u>Extra</u>: Answers will vary.

Hidden Numbers (cont.)

PROBLEMS	WORKSPACE
4. Ann spent a quarter for candy and a dime for gum. How much money did she spend?	
5. Bess wants to buy a book that costs 79¢. She has a half-dollar. How much more money does she need to buy the book?	
6. Matt worked a half hour on his math homework and 20 minutes on his reading home-work. How much time did he spend on his homework?	

Extra: Write some story problems of your own with "hidden number" words. Solve the problems.

FACTS IN PICTURES

Sometimes the facts you need to solve a problem
are given in a picture.

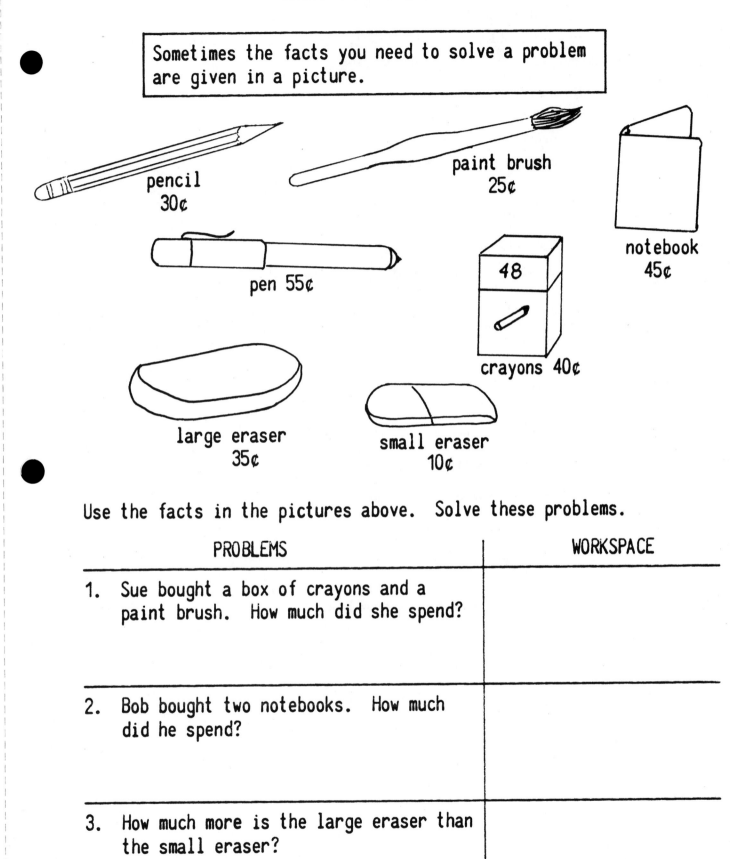

pencil
30¢

paint brush
25¢

notebook
45¢

pen 55¢

48

crayons 40¢

large eraser
35¢

small eraser
10¢

Use the facts in the pictures above. Solve these problems.

PROBLEMS	WORKSPACE
1. Sue bought a box of crayons and a paint brush. How much did she spend?	
2. Bob bought two notebooks. How much did he spend?	
3. How much more is the large eraser than the small eraser?	

Facts In Pictures

Mathematics teaching objectives:

. Solve word problems in which some of the facts are given in pictures.

. Compute with money amounts.

Problem-solving skills pupils might use:

. Guess and check.

. Use an organized list.

. Use math symbols to translate and solve a problem.

Materials needed:

. None

Comments and suggestions:

. Pupils should be able to complete this page after a brief introduction to the directions.

. Problems 6 and 7 are best solved by a "guess and check" strategy. Be sure to discuss how the pupils determined the answers to these problems. Also, note that these problems have more than one right answer.

Answers:

1. 65¢   2. 90¢   3. 25¢   4. 85¢   5. 15¢

6. pencil and paint brush or notebook and small eraser

7. notebook and pencil and small eraser
          or
   crayons and large eraser and small eraser
          or
   large eraser and two paint brushes
          or
   two pencils and a paint brush

Extra: See problem 7 above for answers.

Facts In Pictures (cont.)

PROBLEMS	WORKSPACE
4. Alan bought two pencils and a paint brush. How much did he spend?	
5. Mary wants to buy a box of crayons. She has 25¢. How much more money does she need?	
6. Larry spent 55¢ and bought two things. What did he buy? _____ and _____	
7. Carlos spent 85¢ and bought 3 things. What did he buy? _____ and _____ _____	

Extra: Find as many _different_ solutions as you can to problem 7. Record each below.

FACTS IN A PICTURE

 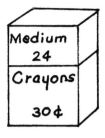 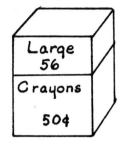

Use the facts in the pictures above to solve these problems.

PROBLEMS	WORKSPACE
1. Sue bought a small box and a medium box of crayons. How much did Sue spend?	
2. Tom bought a medium box and a large box of crayons. How many crayons did Tom buy?	
3. Carol bought 34 crayons. She bought a medium box and a _____ box.	
4. Lee bought two boxes of crayons and spent 45¢. Which two boxes did Lee buy? _____ and _____	
5. Todd bought two boxes of crayons and spent 60¢. Which two boxes did Todd buy? _____ and _____	
6. Mark gave the clerk 25¢ for a box of crayons and got a dime in change. Which box of crayons did Mark buy? _____	

Facts In A Picture

Mathematics teaching objectives:

- Solve word problems in which some of the facts are given in a picture.
- Compute with money amounts.

Problem-solving skills pupils *might* use:

- Guess and check.
- Use math symbols to translate and solve a problem.

Materials needed:

- None

Comments and suggestions:

- Call pupils' attention to the facts given in the picture on the worksheet. Ask pupils to use these facts to solve the problems on the page. Remind them that it may be necessary to "try out" some possible answers (guess and check) in order to solve some examples.

- Discuss solutions and solution strategies when most pupils have completed the page.

- If some pupils have time, let them create word problems to share with their classmates.

Answers:

1. 45¢

2. 80 crayons

3. small

4. small and medium

5. medium and medium

6. small (or 15¢ size)

FACTS IN TABLES

> Sometimes the facts you need to solve a problem
> are given in a table.

This table tells about a library book contest. Use the table to answer the questions below.

Name	Number of Books Read
Bob	6
Carol	11
Ted	8
Alice	10

1. How many books did Ted read? _____

2. Who read ten books? _____

3. Who read the most books? _____

4. How many books did Bob and Carol read altogether? _____

5. Which two persons read 19 books in all? _____ and _____

6. How many books did the two boys read? _____

7. Who read more books in all, the boys or the girls? _____
   How many more? _____

Extra: Make up and record your own word problems that can be solved by using the table. Solve the problems.

Facts In Tables

Mathematics teaching objectives:

. Solve word problems in which some of the facts are given in a table.

Problem-solving skills pupils might use:

. Use an organized list (table).

. Guess and check.

. Use math symbols to translate and solve a problem.

Materials needed:

. None

Comments and suggestions:

. Call pupils' attention to the table they will need to use to solve the problems on this page. Have them complete the page on their own.

. Discuss and compare answers when most pupils have finished.

. Let pupils who have created their own word problems share them.

Answers:

1. 8

2. Alice

3. Carol

4. 17

5. Carol and Ted

6. 14

7. girls
7 more books

MAKE-BELIEVE ANIMALS

Sometimes you can make a drawing to solve a problem.

Make a drawing to solve each problem.

PROBLEM	WORKSPACE	ANSWER
1. A fleek has 2 heads. How many heads on 4 fleeks?		
2. A mook has 5 legs. How many legs on 3 mooks?		
3. A muk has 3 tails. How many tails on four muks?		
4. Each burt has four wings. How many wings on two burts?		
5. Each flook has three horns. How many horns on 3 flooks?		
6. Each chack has 4 legs. How many legs on four chacks?		
7. Each munck has 4 arms with three fingers on each arm. How many fingers does each munck have?		

Extra: Write/your own "make-believe animal" word problems. Solve.

<u>Make-Believe Animals</u>

Mathematics teaching objectives:

. Solve word problems by making a drawing.

. Recognize that word problems can be solved in a variety of ways.

Problem-solving skills pupils <u>might</u> use:

. Make a drawing.

. Use math symbols to translate and solve a problem.

Materials needed:

. None

Comments and suggestions:

. Distribute worksheet. Suggest pupils use drawings (simplified stick-type are O.K.) to solve the problems.

. When most pupils have completed the page, discuss answers.

. Discuss other possible ways to solve each problem (add or multiply) for example.

. Share any problems created by pupils in the Extra activity.

Answers:

1. 8 heads

2. 15 legs

3. 12 tails

4. 8 wings

5. 9 horns

6. 16 legs

7. 12 fingers

Extra: Answers will vary.

BE REASONABLE!

> Both the number facts and the answer to word problems should be reasonable.

Mike ate _____ apples.
Judy ate _____ apples.
How many more apples did Judy eat than Mike?

1. Can you solve this problem?

   Decide what number facts would be reasonable.

   Fill in the facts.
   Solve the problem.

2. Fill in the blanks below. Solve the problems.

PROBLEMS	WORKSPACE
a. Kay bought ____ tapes at _____ dollars each. How much in all did Kay pay for the tapes?	
b. Rose baked ____ dozen cookies. Carl baked ____ dozen cookies. How many dozen cookies did they make in all?	
c. Lois bought ____ pencils at ____ cents each. How much did the pencils cost in all?	
d. Chad had ____ rabbits. He gave ____ of them to Bob. How many does he have left?	
e. Slim weighs ____ pounds. His father weighs ____ pounds. How much heavier is Slim's father?	
f. Jed spent ____ cents for a pen. Ted spent ____ cents for a pen. How much more did Ted spend than Jed?	
g. Todd bought ____ books. Each cost ____. How much did Todd spend on the books?	

<u>Be Reasonable</u> !

Mathematics teaching objectives:

- Solve addition and subtraction word problems.
- Supply reasonable missing data for word problems.

Problem-solving skills pupils <u>might</u> use:

- Make a reasonable estimate.
- Simplify the problem.
- Use math symbols to translate and solve a problem.

Materials needed:

- None

Comments and suggestions:

- Discuss problem 1 as a class. Have pupils complete the rest of the activity on their own. Remind pupils the numbers they use should be <u>reasonable</u>.
- When most pupils are finished, discuss and compare results.

Answers:

Answers will vary. Accept any <u>reasonable</u> answers that "fit" the problems.

MISSING NUMBER STORIES

Fill in the blanks. Solve each problem. Label your answers.

PROBLEMS	WORKSPACE
1. Mike had 75 goldfish. He bought _____ more. How many goldfish in all?	
2. Carol had _____ cats. 16 cats ran away. How many cats are there now?	
3. George had 48 dollars. He found _____ dollars. How much money does he have in all?	
4. Mary had _____ dollars. She spent 17 dollars. How much change did she get?	
5. Dan bought 24 ice cream bars. He ate _____ of them. How many are left?	
6. Mark picked 76 apples. He ate _____ apples. How many are left?	
7. Tony had 61 toy cars. He bought _____ more. How many cars is this in all?	
8. Maria had 64 marbles. She gave _____ away. How many marbles were left?	
9. Steve had _____ books. He bought 3 more. How many books is this in all?	

Missing Number Stories

Mathematics teaching objectives:

- Solve addition and subtraction word problems.
- Supply reasonable missing data for word problems.

Problem-solving skills pupils might use:

- Make a reasonable estimate.

Materials needed:

- None

Comments and suggestions:

- Distribute worksheets. Have pupils complete the problems on their own. Remind them that their answers should be reasonable and should "fit" the story. Discuss and compare answers when most pupils have completed the page.

- Pupils who finish ahead of others might be asked to make up other missing number stories to use for future worksheets or class activities.

Answers:

Answers will vary. Accept any reasonable answers that "fit" the problems.

HOBBY STORIES

Fill in the blanks. Solve each problem. Label your answers.

PROBLEMS	WORKSPACE
1. Ann collects insects. She has ____ beetles and ____ ants in a case. How many insects are in the case?	
2. Ann's brother Rex likes insects too. His largest set contains ____ butterflies and ____ moths. How many are in this set?	
3. Gloria collects miniature toy cats and horses. She has ____ cats and ____ horses. How many toy animals does she have in all?	
4. Duane loves dogs. He has ____ wooden dogs, ____ china dogs, and ____ metal dogs. How many toy dogs does Duane have in his collection?	
5. Cheryl collects stuffed animals. She has ____ dogs, ____ bears, ____ cats, a tiger, a fox, a monkey, a turtle, and a very long snake. How many stuffed animals does Cheryl have?	

Extra: Make up and solve other "hobby stories."

<u>Hobby</u> <u>Stories</u>

Mathematics teaching objectives:

　• Supply missing data and solve addition and subtraction word problems.

Problem-solving skills pupils <u>might</u> use:

　• Make a reasonable estimate.

　• Use math symbols to translate and solve a problem.

Materials needed:

　• None

Comments and suggestions:

　• Encourage pupils to supply <u>reasonable</u> data.

　• Discuss and compare answers when most pupils have completed the page.

　• Share any problems created by pupils.

Answers:

　Answers will vary. Accept any that are reasonable and "fit" the problem.

SHORT STORIES

All the facts in a word problem should make sense.

Read these problems carefully. Fill in the blanks. Solve each problem. Label your answers.

PROBLEMS	WORKSPACE
1. Lee had 43 _____ . She gave 14 away. How many were left?	
2. Tom saw 38 _____ . 13 flew aways. How many were left?	
3. 34 _____ butterflies. 28 _____ butterflies. How many butterflies in all?	
4. 26 dogs. 42 _____ How many animals in all?	
5. 42 _____ . 35 ran away. How many were left?	
6. Mike had 44 dollars. He spent 5 _____ . How much money was left?	
7. 61 fleas. 17 _____ How many insects in all?	

© PSM 82

-139-

<u>Short</u> <u>Stories</u>

Mathematics teaching objectives:

- Create and solve addition and subtraction word problems.
- Compute with money amounts.

Problem-solving skills pupils <u>might</u> use:

- Use math symbols to translate and solve a problem.

Materials needed:

- None

Comments and suggestions:

- Encourage pupils to supply <u>reasonable</u> data.
- Discuss and compare answers when most pupils have completed the page.
- Share any problems created by pupils.

Answers:

Answers will vary. Accept any that are reasonable and "fit" the problem.

FILL IN THE BLANKS

Read carefully. Fill in the blanks. Solve each problem. Label your answers.

PROBLEMS	WORKSPACE
1. Bob saw 93 _____. 23 of them ran away. How many stayed?	
2. Lee had 95 _____. She ate 23 of them. How many were left?	
3. Jill paid 73 dollars for a _____. She paid 13 dollars for a _____. How much did she spend?	
4. Carlos has 116 _____ and 38 _____. How many animals in all does he have?	
5. There are 78 _____ on a shelf. There are 96 _____ on the other shelf. How many are there in all?	
6. Nancy collected 183 _____. Seven of them were broken. How many of them were not?	

Extra: Write some word problems for your classmates
        to "finish" and solve.

Fill In The Blanks

Mathematics teaching objectives:

- Create and solve addition and subtraction word problems.
- Compute with money amounts.

Problem-solving skills pupils <u>might</u> use:

- Use math symbols to translate and solve a problem.

Materials needed:

- None

Comments and suggestions:

- Encourage pupils to supply reasonable data.
- Discuss and compare answers when most pupils have completed the page.
- Share any problems created by pupils.

Answers:

Missing data supplied to the problems will vary. Therefore the <u>labels</u> to some of the answers will vary. Correct numerical answers are as follows:

1. 70 _____
2. 72 _____
3. $86
4. 154 animals
5. 174 _____
6. 176 _____

WHAT'S MISSING?

Read carefully. Fill in the blanks. Solve each problem. Label your answers.

PROBLEMS	WORKSPACE
1. Ann had 29 _____. She got 18 more. How many does she have now?	
2. Beth got two _____. Each cost 19 dollars. How much for both?	
3. Sue had 72 _____. She ate five. How many are left?	
4. Mike had 41 _____. He gave away sixteen. How many did he keep?	
5. Fran had 43 _____. Seventeen of them popped. How many did not pop?	
6. Thirty chairs are in the room. Sixteen _____ are in chairs. How many chairs are empty?	
7. Rosa had 37 _____. She and Mary each ate one. How many were left?	
8. Each _____ costs 27 dollars. How much for two_____?	

What's Missing?

Mathematics teaching objectives:

- Create and solve addition and subtraction word problems.
- Compute with money amounts.

Problem-solving skills pupils might use:

- Use math symbols to translate and solve a problem.

Materials needed:

- None

Comments and suggestions:

- Encourage pupils to supply reasonable data.
- Discuss and compare answers when most pupils have completed the page.
- Share any problems created by pupils.

Answers:

Missing data supplied to the problems will vary. Therefore, the labels to some of the answers will vary. Correct numerical answers are as follows:

1. 47 _____
2. 38 _____
3. 67 _____
4. 25 _____
5. 14 chairs
6. 35 _____
7. $54

YOU ASK THE QUESTIONS

A word problem gives some facts and asks a question.
To solve the problem, you find and answer the question.

1. Can you solve this problem?

   What is missing?

   Write a question for the problem. Solve the problem.

   Art read 36 pages of a book. Lee read 78 pages.

   _____

   _____

   _____

2. Write a question for each problem below. Solve the problems.

PROBLEMS	WORKSPACE
a. Joe has 28 model planes. Sue has 16 model planes. _____ _____ _____	
b. Randy took 32 pictures on vacation. Bob took 12 pictures. _____ _____ _____	
c. May spent $28 for a radio and $5 for a game. _____ _____ _____ _____	

Mathematics teaching objectives:

  . Create and solve addition and subtraction word problems.

  . Compute with money amounts.

Problem-solving skills pupils <u>might</u> use:

  . Use math symbols to translate and solve a problem.

Materials needed:

  . None

Comments and suggestions:

  . Discuss problem 1. Let several pupils suggest possible questions to go
    with the word problem. Have pupils complete the rest of the problems
    on their own.

  . When most pupils have completed the activity, discuss and compare questions
    and solutions.

Answers:

  Answers will vary. Accept any reasonable questions and the correct
  matching solutions.

PROBLEMS	WORKSPACE
d. Pat had 28¢. Her father gave her 52¢. _____ _____ _____ _____ _____	
e. Chris baked 6 dozen coconut cookies and 8 dozen chocolate chip cookies. _____ _____ _____ _____	
f. A notebook costs 60¢. An eraser costs 35¢. _____ _____ _____ _____	
g. Susan read 61 pages of a book. There are 85 pages in all in the book. _____ _____ _____	
h. Mark earned 12 dollars on Friday and 10 dollars on Saturday. _____ _____ _____	

WHAT'S NOT NEEDED?

> Some word problems give more facts than you need to solve the problem.

Cross out the information that is not needed to solve the problems below. Then solve the problems.

PROBLEMS	WORKSPACE
1. Anna has 16 pets. Cathy has 5 pets. Mike has a dog and cat. How many more pets does Anna have than Cathy?	
2. Maria bought a bracelet for $8 and a ring for $21. She saw a necklace that cost $25. How much money did she spend?	
3. Bill has 13 cats. Jill has 6 cats. Judy has 12 cats. How many cats do Bill and Judy have?	
4. Josh walked 10 kilometers on his birth-day. He is fifteen years old. José is 9 years old. How much older is Josh than José ?	
5. Pete bought six candy bars for 25 cents each. Mack bought four candy bars for 20 cents each. How much money did Mack spend?	
6. Beth has 8 dollars in her piggy bank. She bought a kite that cost $2 and a book that cost five dollars. How much money did she spend?	

What's Not Needed?

Mathematics teaching objectives:

- Recognize and solve word problems with extraneous information.
- Compute with money amounts.

Problem-solving skills pupils _might_ use:

- Eliminate (or ignore) data not needed.
- Use math symbols to translate and solve a problem.

Materials needed:

- None

Comments and suggestions:

- Discuss problem 1 as a class. Have pupils complete the rest of the page on their own.
- Discuss the problems when most pupils have completed the activity.
- Pupils who finish ahead of others might be asked to make up other problems to share.

Answers:

1.	Mike has a dog and a cat.	11 pets
2.	She saw a necklace that cost $25.	$29
3.	Jill has 6 cats.	25 cats
4.	Josh walked 10 kilometers on his birthday.	6 years
5.	Pete bought six candy bars for 25 cents each.	80¢
6.	Beth has 8 dollars in her piggy bank.	$7

HIDDEN QUESTIONS

A word problem gives some facts and asks a question. Some of the number facts may be "hidden." To finish these problems you must first find and solve the hidden question.

Read and discuss this problem.

- What is the hidden number word?
- Which hidden question do you first solve before finishing the problem?
- What is the answer to the problem?

> Lou had two dozen pens. She gave 18 of them to Lee. How many pens does Lou have now?

PROBLEM	WORKSPACE	
	Hidden Problem	Solution
1. Betty has two quarters. Joe has 78¢. How much more money does Joe have than Betty?		
2. John has 3 dozen marbles. Jess gave him 11 more. How many marbles does John have now?		
3. Luke worked 2 hours in the garden and 35 minutes on the lawn. How many minutes did he work in all?		

Mathematics teaching objectives:

. Recognize and solve simple two-step word problems.

. Compute with money amounts.

Problem-solving skills pupils might use:

. Use math symbols to translate and solve a problem.

Materials needed:

. None

Comments and suggestions:

. Read the problem in the "cloud." Find the hidden number word (dozen) and discuss the solution of the problem. Pupils can then complete the activity on their own.

. Pupils who wish to do so should be encouraged to share the "hidden question" word problem they have created.

Answers:

1. Hidden problem: 2 x 25¢ = 50¢
    Answers: 28¢

2. Hidden problem: 3 x 12 = 36
    Answers: 47 marbles

3. Hidden problem: 2 x 60 = 120 minutes
    Answers: 155 minutes

4. Hidden questions: 3 x 10¢ = 30¢
                       30¢ and 5¢ = 35¢
    Answer: 40¢

5. Hidden questions: 3 yards + 1 yard = 4 yards
                       4 x 3 feet = 12 feet
    Answer: 14 feet

6. Hidden question: Each car needs 4 (or 5) tires.
    Answer: 12 (or 15) tires.

Extra: Answers will vary.

PROBLEMS	WORKSPACE	
	Hidden Problems	Solution
4. Dick has 3 dimes and a nickel. He wants to buy a book that costs 75¢. How much more money does he need?		
5. Mark dug 3 yards of ditch on Monday, 1 yard on Tuesday, and 2 feet on Wednesday. How many feet of ditch did he dig?		
6. The Johnsons have 3 cars. Each car needs all new tires. How many tires will they need to buy?		

Extra: Write several problems of your own with "hidden number" words. Solve the problems.

1. Solve these problems.

    a. You have $.35
        You spend $.24
        You have _____ left.

    b. You have $.65.
        You spend $.46.
        You have _____ left.

    c. You have a quarter.
        You spend $.18.
        You have _____ left.

    d. You have 2 quarters.
        You spend $.43.
        You have _____ left.

    e. You have a half-dollar.
        You spend a nickel.
        You have _____ left.

    f. You have a quarter and a dime.
        You spend $.28.
        You have _____ left.

2. Fill in the blanks. Finish each problem.

    a. You have a quarter and 3 nickels.
        You spend _____.
        You have _____ left.

    b. You have a half-dollar, 2 dimes and 1 nickel.
        You spend _____.
        You have _____ left.

    c. You have _____ quarters.
        You spend $.39.
        You have _____ left.

    d. You have _____.
        You spend _____.
        You have $.01 left.

    e. You have _____.
        You spend _____.
        You have $.17 left.

How Much Is Left?

Mathematics teaching objectives:

. Practice with mental addition and subtraction of 2-digit numbers.

. Practice applying mathematics to read world situations.

. Practice using coin values (quarter, nickel, dime, penny).

. Practice creating "word-type" problems.

. Practice with 2-step word problems.

Problem-solving skills pupils might use:

. Guess and check.

. Work backwards.

Materials needed:

. None

Comments and suggestions:

. Work parts a, b, c, and d of part 1 as a class activity. (Pupils may need to discuss the "hidden question" in part d, namely, What is the value of two quarters?) Pupils should be able to complete the remainder of the page on their own. Some pupils may need assurance that it is O.K. to make up any reasonable numbers to complete problems in part 2.

. Be sure to allow time to discuss the various problems created by pupils in part 2. It is important that pupils recognize that many math problems can have more than one right answer.

Answers:

1. a. $.11   b. $.19   c. $.07   d. $.07   e. $.45   f. $.07

2. a-e. Answers will vary. Accept any reasonable answers.

WHAT'S LEFT ?

1. Solve these problems.

   a. You have 25¢.
      You spend 17¢.
      You have _____ left.

   b. You have $.75.
      You spend $.58.
      You have _____ left.

   c. You have a quarter.
      You spend 17¢.
      You have _____ left.

   d. You have a half-dollar.
      You spend $.38.
      You have _____ left.

   e. You have a quarter and a dime.
      You spend $.28.
      You have _____ left.

   f. You have a quarter and 3 nickels.
      You spend $.39.
      You have _____ left.

   g. You have a half-dollar, 2 dimes, and 2 nickels.
      You spend $.76.
      You have _____ left.

2. Fill in the blanks. Finish each problem.

   a. You have a half dollar.
      You spend _____.
      You have _____ left.

   b. You have _____ dimes.
      You spend $.37.
      You have _____ left.

   c. You have one quarter and __ dimes.
      You spend _____.
      You have _____ left.

   d. You have ___ dimes and 2 pennies.
      You spend _____.
      You have _____ left.

   e. You have _____.
      You spend _____.
      You have $.10 left.

   f. You have _____.
      You spend _____.
      You have $.27 left.

What's Left?

Mathematics teaching objectives:

. Practice with mental addition and subtraction of 2-digit numbers (money values).

. Practice applying mathematics to real world situations.

. Practice using coin values (half-dollar, quarter, dime, nickel, penny).

. Practice creating "story-type" problems.

. Have informal practice with 2-step story problems.

Problem-solving skills pupils might use:

. Guess and check.

. Work backwards.

Materials:

. None

Comments and suggestions:

. Work parts a, b, and c of the first activity as a class. Discuss the need to "change" some coin names into coin values in order to solve part c. Point out that other problems on this page have similar "hidden questions." Pupils should be able to complete the remainder of the page on their own or by working with a partner.

. Some pupils may need assurance that it is "O.K." to make up any reasonable numbers to complete the problems in the second activity. It is important that pupils recognize that many math problems can have more than one right answer.

. Be sure to give pupils who wish to do so an opportunity to share the problems they created in no. 2.

Answers:

1. a. 8¢   b. 17¢   c. 8¢   d. 12¢   e. 7¢   f. 1¢   g. 4¢

2. a-f. Answers will vary.

HEADLINES

Write a word problem to match each "headline" below.

HEADLINE	MY WORD PROBLEM
23 + 18 41 chairs	
$ 1.25 + .16 1.41	
48 - 12 36 cupcakes	
16 3 + 29 48 records	
142 - 116 26 jelly beans	
47 - 13 34 dinosaurs	

Headlines

Mathematics teaching objectives:

. Create addition and subtraction story problems.

Problem-solving skills pupils _might_ use:

. Invent a problem situation for a mathematical expression.

Materials needed:

. None

Comments and suggestions:

. If pupils have not had many opportunities to create word problems of their own, make up several "headlines" and have them suggest different word problems that would be solved by each. Once pupils understand the idea, have them complete the page on their own.

. Pupils who finish ahead of others might be asked to make up additional headlines that would make good word problems.

. The most important part of this activity is the "sharing" of completed pupil word problems. Allow plenty of time for sharing and discussion.

Answers:

Answers will vary.

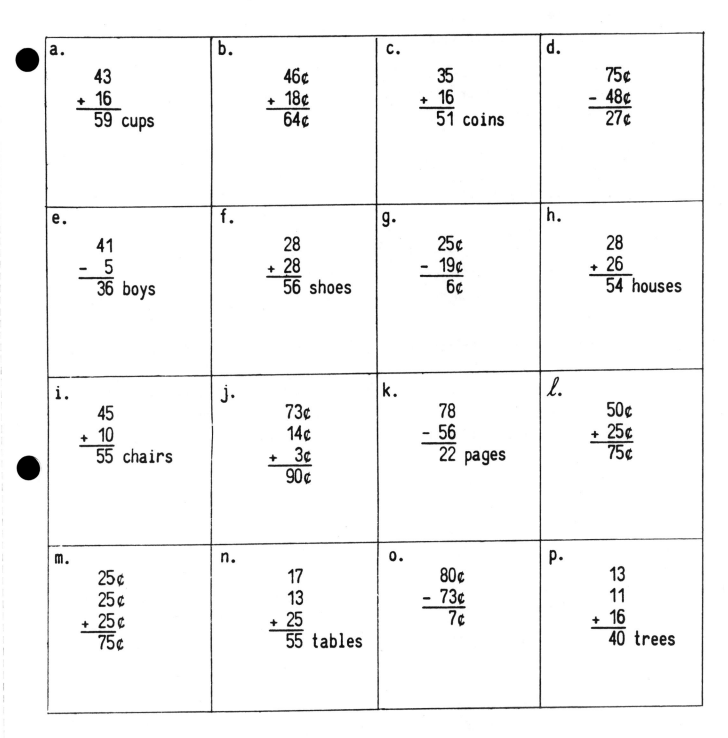

a. $\begin{array}{r} 43 \\ +\ 16 \\ \hline 59 \end{array}$ cups	**b.** $\begin{array}{r} 46¢ \\ +\ 18¢ \\ \hline 64¢ \end{array}$	**c.** $\begin{array}{r} 35 \\ +\ 16 \\ \hline 51 \end{array}$ coins	**d.** $\begin{array}{r} 75¢ \\ -\ 48¢ \\ \hline 27¢ \end{array}$
e. $\begin{array}{r} 41 \\ -\ 5 \\ \hline 36 \end{array}$ boys	**f.** $\begin{array}{r} 28 \\ +\ 28 \\ \hline 56 \end{array}$ shoes	**g.** $\begin{array}{r} 25¢ \\ -\ 19¢ \\ \hline 6¢ \end{array}$	**h.** $\begin{array}{r} 28 \\ +\ 26 \\ \hline 54 \end{array}$ houses
i. $\begin{array}{r} 45 \\ +\ 10 \\ \hline 55 \end{array}$ chairs	**j.** $\begin{array}{r} 73¢ \\ 14¢ \\ +\ 3¢ \\ \hline 90¢ \end{array}$	**k.** $\begin{array}{r} 78 \\ -\ 56 \\ \hline 22 \end{array}$ pages	**ℓ.** $\begin{array}{r} 50¢ \\ +\ 25¢ \\ \hline 75¢ \end{array}$
m. $\begin{array}{r} 25¢ \\ 25¢ \\ +\ 25¢ \\ \hline 75¢ \end{array}$	**n.** $\begin{array}{r} 17 \\ 13 \\ +\ 25 \\ \hline 55 \end{array}$ tables	**o.** $\begin{array}{r} 80¢ \\ -\ 73¢ \\ \hline 7¢ \end{array}$	**p.** $\begin{array}{r} 13 \\ 11 \\ +\ 16 \\ \hline 40 \end{array}$ trees

Play one side of the room against the other, using a transparency of
   this page and an overhead projector.
Take turns. Pick any square. Give a story problem that could be
   solved by using the problem in that square. If correct, mark the
   square with your mark (X or O).
Winner is the first side to get 3 marks in a row, column, or diagonal.

Headline <u>Tic-Tac-Toe</u> - <u>A</u>

Mathematics teaching objectives:

. Create addition and subtraction word problems.

Problem-solving skills pupils <u>might</u> use:

. Search printed materials for needed information.

. Create a problem which can be solved by certain solution procedures.

Materials needed:

. Overhead transparency of the activity page

. Overhead projector

Comments and suggestions:

. Use this as a whole-class activity. Display the gameboard (activity sheet) on the overhead projector screen or on the chalkboard.

. Take turns calling on various pupils, alternating sides of the room (X and O sides).

. The object of the activity is to get <u>three</u> marks in a row, column, or diagonal.

. This activity can be used over and over again until pupils "discover" the first team can always win in 5 moves by choosing one of the four center squares. It is a good "time filler" for use when you have a few spare minutes.

Answers:

Answers will vary.

HEADLINE TIC-TAC-TOE - B

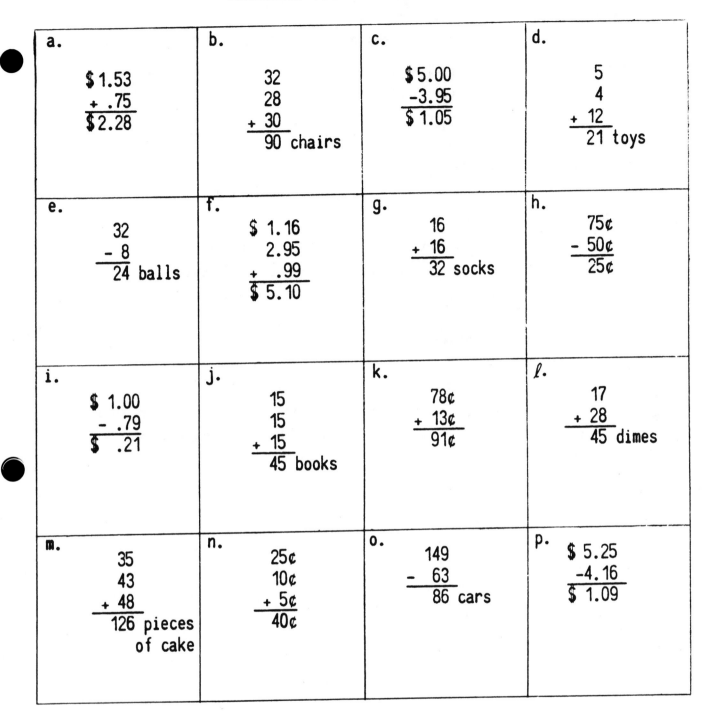

a. $\begin{array}{r} \$1.53 \\ +\ .75 \\ \hline \$2.28 \end{array}$	b. $\begin{array}{r} 32 \\ 28 \\ +\ 30 \\ \hline 90 \end{array}$ chairs	c. $\begin{array}{r} \$5.00 \\ -3.95 \\ \hline \$1.05 \end{array}$	d. $\begin{array}{r} 5 \\ 4 \\ +\ 12 \\ \hline 21 \end{array}$ toys
e. $\begin{array}{r} 32 \\ -\ 8 \\ \hline 24 \end{array}$ balls	f. $\begin{array}{r} \$1.16 \\ 2.95 \\ +\ .99 \\ \hline \$5.10 \end{array}$	g. $\begin{array}{r} 16 \\ +\ 16 \\ \hline 32 \end{array}$ socks	h. $\begin{array}{r} 75\cancel{c} \\ -\ 50\cancel{c} \\ \hline 25\cancel{c} \end{array}$
i. $\begin{array}{r} \$1.00 \\ -\ .79 \\ \hline \$\ .21 \end{array}$	j. $\begin{array}{r} 15 \\ 15 \\ +\ 15 \\ \hline 45 \end{array}$ books	k. $\begin{array}{r} 78\cancel{c} \\ +\ 13\cancel{c} \\ \hline 91\cancel{c} \end{array}$	l. $\begin{array}{r} 17 \\ +\ 28 \\ \hline 45 \end{array}$ dimes
m. $\begin{array}{r} 35 \\ 43 \\ +\ 48 \\ \hline 126 \end{array}$ pieces of cake	n. $\begin{array}{r} 25\cancel{c} \\ 10\cancel{c} \\ +\ 5\cancel{c} \\ \hline 40\cancel{c} \end{array}$	o. $\begin{array}{r} 149 \\ -\ 63 \\ \hline 86 \end{array}$ cars	p. $\begin{array}{r} \$5.25 \\ -4.16 \\ \hline \$1.09 \end{array}$

Play one side of the room against the other, using a transparency of
    this page and an overhead projector.
Take turns. Pick any square. Give a story problem that could be
    solved by using the problem in that square. If correct, mark the
    square with your mark (X or O).
Winner is the first side to get 3 marks in a row, column, or diagonal.

Mathematics teaching objectives:

. Create addition and subtraction word problems.

Problem-solving skills pupils <u>might</u> use:

. Search printed materials for needed information.

. Create a problem which can be solved by certain solution procedures.

Materials needed:

. Overhead transparency of the activity page

. Overhead projector

Comments and suggestions:

. Use this as a whole-class activity. Display the gameboard (activity sheet) on the overhead projector screen or on the chalkboard.

. Take turns calling on various pupils, alternating sides of the room (X and 0 sides).

. The object of the activity is to get <u>three</u> marks in a row, column, or diagonal.

. This activity can be used over and over again until pupils "discover" the first team can always win in 5 moves by choosing one of the four center squares. It is a good "time filler" for use when you have a few spare minutes.

Answers:

Answers will vary.

a. 73 + 49 ——— 122 pupils	**b.** $ 4.50 + .16 ——— $ 4.66	**c.** 146 - 16 ——— 130 days	**d.** $ 9.95 + 2.98 ——— $12.93
e. $ 5.00 - 4.49 ——— $ .51	**f.** 46 + 92 ——— 138 cars	**g.** $ 10.00 - 6.98 ——— $ 3.02	**h.** 39 37 + 35 ——— 111 rooms
i. 93 + 16 ——— 109 pictures	**j.** $ 4.50 2.98 + 6.50 ——— $13.98	**k.** 26 13 + 18 ——— 57 books	**ℓ.** $ 3.50 + 3.50 ——— $ 7.00
m. $ 9.00 - 6.50 ——— $ 2.50	**n.** 170 - 3 ——— 167 days	**o.** $ 12.00 - 11.98 ——— $ .02	**p.** 525 - 516 ——— 9 pieces of pie

Play one side of the room against the other, using a transparency of this page and an overhead projector.

Take turns. Pick any square. Give a story problem that could be solved by using the problem in that square. If correct, mark the square with your mark (X or O).

Winner is the first side to get 3 marks in a row, column, or diagonal.

Mathematics teaching objectives:

. Create addition and subtraction word problems.

Problem-solving skills pupils <u>might</u> use:

. Search printed materials for needed information.

. Create a problem which can be solved by certain solution procedures.

Materials needed:

. Overhead transparency of the activity page

. Overhead projector

Comments and suggestions:

. Use this as a whole-class activity. Display the gameboard (activity
  sheet) on the overhead projector screen or on the chalkboard.

. Take turns calling on various pupils, alternating sides of the room
  (X and 0 sides).

. The object of the activity is to get <u>three</u> marks in a row, column, or
  diagonal.

. This activity can be used over and over again until pupils "discover"
  the first team can always win in 5 moves by choosing one of the four
  center squares. It is a good "time filler" for use when you have a
  few spare minutes.

Answers:

Answers will vary.

III. TANGRAMS

TANGRAM PIECES PATTERN

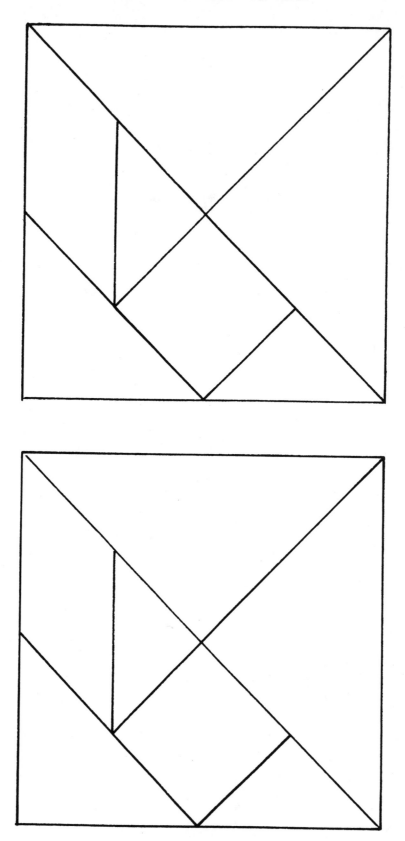

© PSM 82

TANGRAMS - A

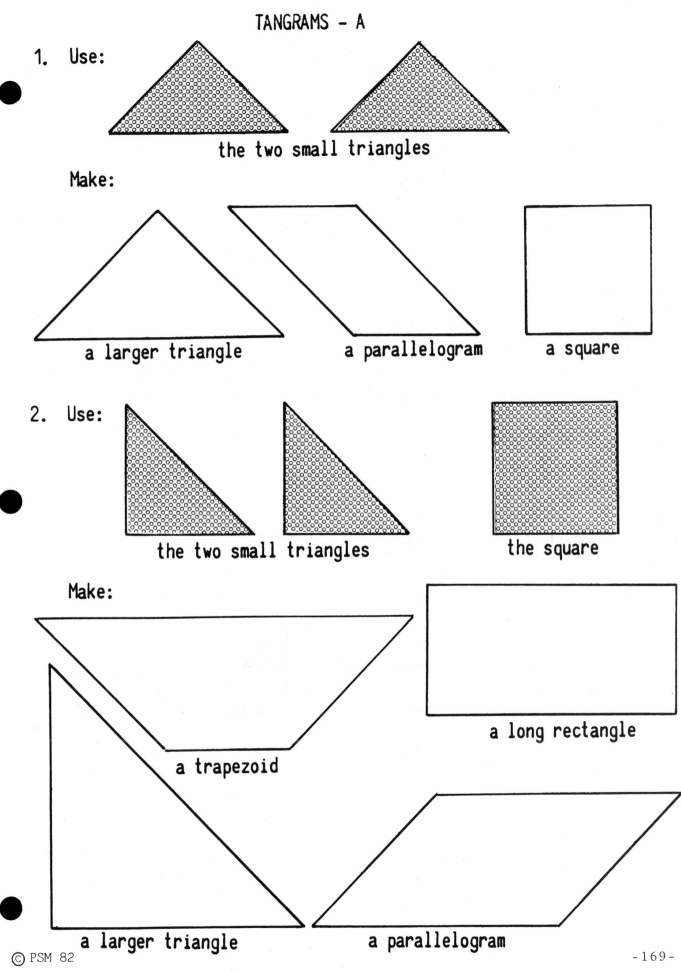

1. Use:

the two small triangles

Make:

a larger triangle

a parallelogram

a square

2. Use:

the two small triangles

the square

Make:

a trapezoid

a long rectangle

a larger triangle

a parallelogram

Tangrams - A

Mathematics teaching objectives:

- Recognize polygons (triangle, square, parallelogram, rectangle, trapezoid).
- Recognize and use relationships between and among polygons.
- Provide informal tessellation experiences.

Problem-solving skills pupils might use:

- Make a model.
- Guess and check.

Materials needed:

- One set of tangram pieces for each pupil (reproduced on tag or coverstock, using the pattern on page 168).

Comments and suggestions:

- Do the shapes in part 1 as a whole-class activity. Have pupils record their results by tracing the pieces used to cover the shapes on the worksheet.
- Pupils can complete the rest of the page on their own or by working with a partner. All results should be recorded, as suggested above.
- Pupils who finish ahead of others can create other polygons or designs using the tangram pieces.

Answers:

1.

2.

Use:

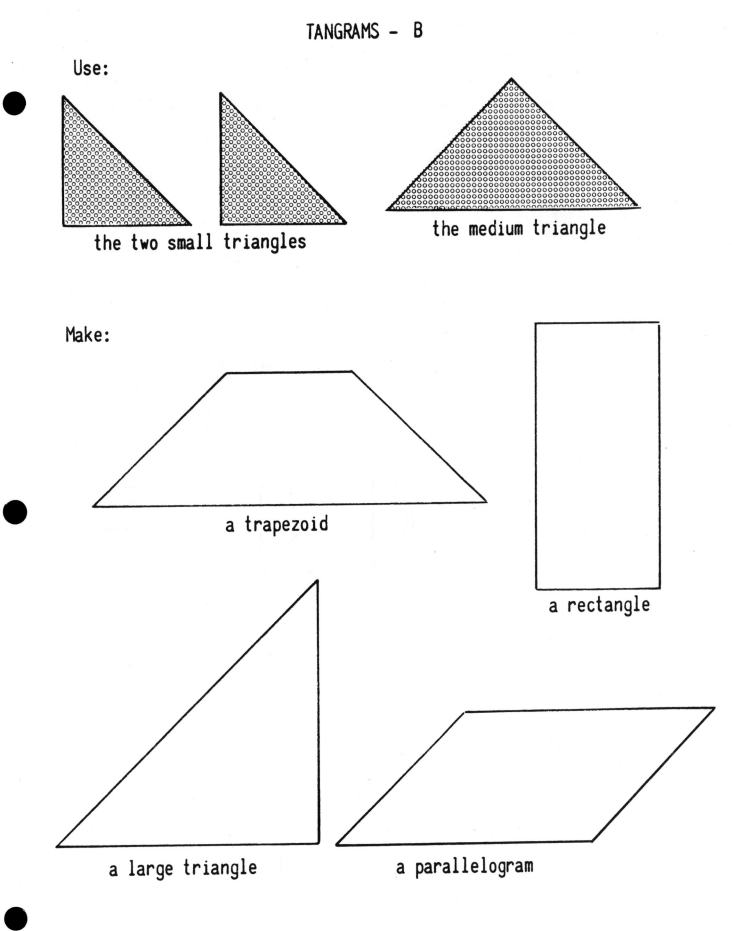

the two small triangles

the medium triangle

Make:

a trapezoid

a rectangle

a large triangle

a parallelogram

Tangrams - <u>B</u>

Mathematics teaching objectives:

- Recognize certain polygons (rectangle, trapezoid, triangle, parallelogram).
- Recognize and use relationships between and among certain polygons.
- Provide informal tessellation experiences.

Problem-solving skills pupils <u>might</u> use:

- Make a model.
- Guess and check.

Materials needed:

- One set of tangram pieces for each pupil (reproduced on tag or coverstock using the pattern on page 168).

Comments and suggestions:

- Pupils can complete this activity on their own or by working with a partner. Results are to be recorded by tracing the pieces used to cover the shapes on the worksheet.
- Pupils who complete the activity ahead of others can create other polygons or designs using the tangram pieces.

Answers:

Use:

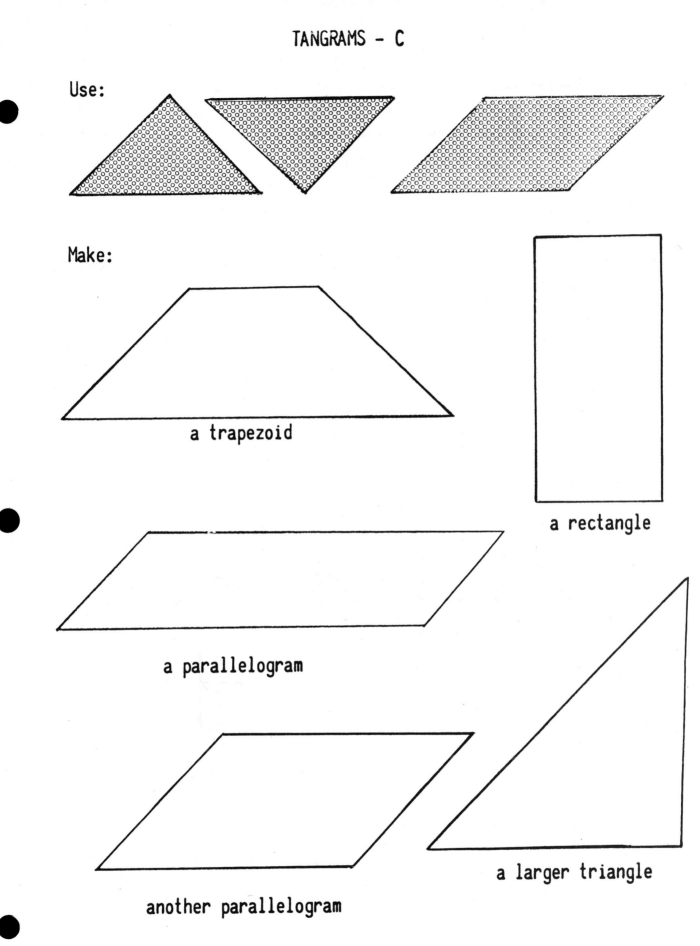

Make:

a trapezoid

a rectangle

a parallelogram

another parallelogram

a larger triangle

Tangrams - C

Mathematics taching objectives:

- Recognize polygons (trapezoid, rectangle, parallelogram, triangle).
- Recognize and use relationships between and among polygons.
- Provide informal tessellation experiences.

Problem-solving skills pupils might use:

- Make a model.
- Guess and check.

Materials needed:

- One set of tangram pieces for each pupil (reproduced on tag or coverstock using the pattern on page 168).

Comments and suggestions:

- Pupils can complete this activity on their own or by working with a partner. Results are to be recorded by tracing the pieces used to cover the shapes on the worksheet.
- Pupils who complete the activity ahead of others can create other polygons or designs using the tangram pieces.
- This activity usually is more difficult for pupils than either of Tangrams - A or Tangrams - B.

Answers:

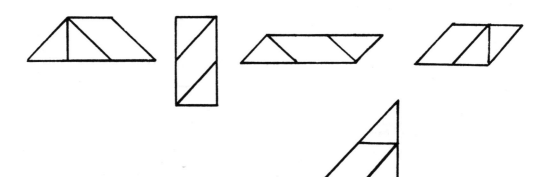

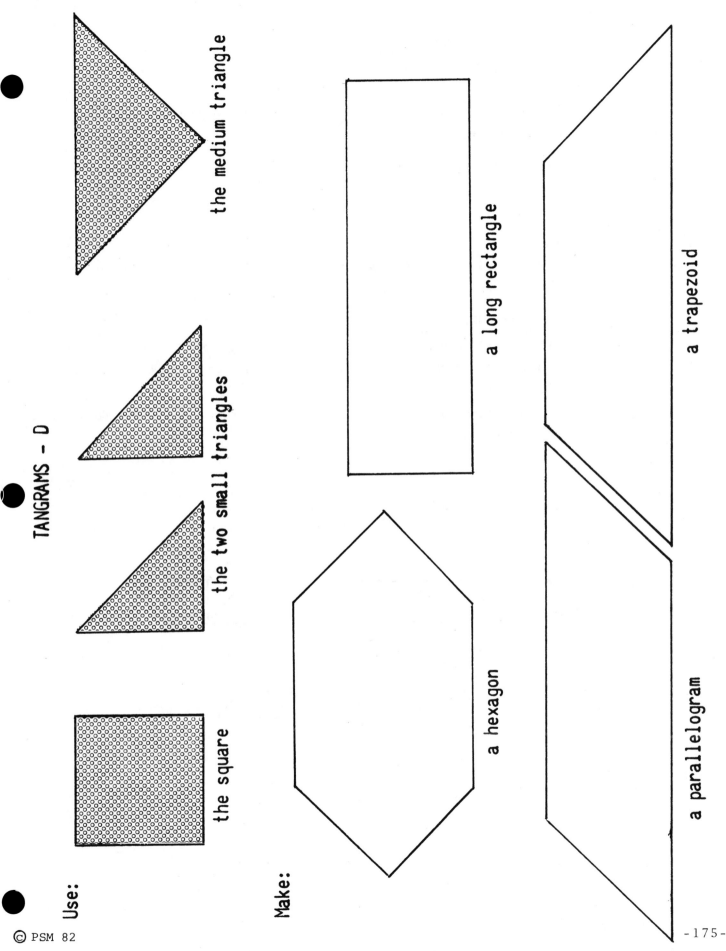

TANGRAMS - D

Use:
the medium triangle
the two small triangles
the square

Make:
a long rectangle
a trapezoid
a hexagon
a parallelogram

© PSM 82

Tangrams - <u>D</u>

Mathematics teaching objectives:

- Recognize polygons (square, triangle, hexagon, rectangle, parallelogram, trapezoid)
- Recognize and use relationships between and among polygons.
- Provide informal tessellation experiences.

Problem-solving skills pupils <u>might</u> use:

- Make a model.
- Guess and check.

Materials needed:

- One set of tangram pieces for each pupil (reproduced on tag or coverstock using the pattern on page 168).

Comments and suggestions:

- Pupils can complete this activity on their own or by working with a partner. Results are to be recorded by <u>tracing</u> the pieces used to cover the shapes on the worksheet.
- Pupils who complete the activity ahead of others can create other polygons or designs using the tangram pieces.

Answers:

Answers can vary. One way for each is shown below.

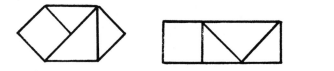

TANGRAMS - E

Use:

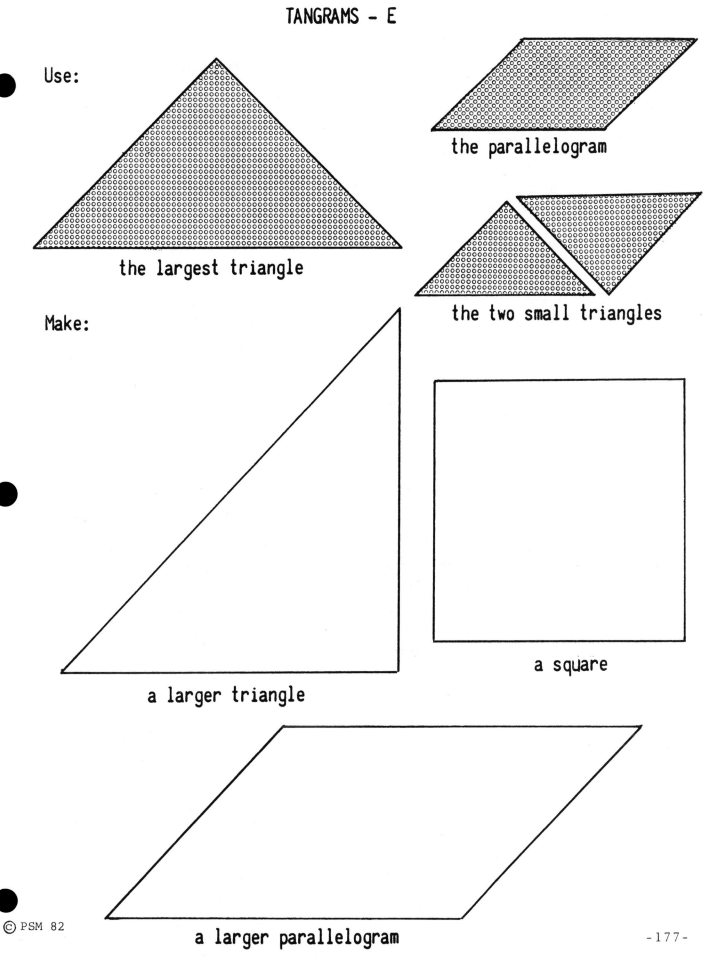

the largest triangle

the parallelogram

the two small triangles

Make:

a larger triangle

a square

a larger parallelogram

Tangrams - E

Mathematics teaching objectives:

- Recognize polygons (square, triangle, hexagon, rectangle, parallelogram, trapezoid).
- Recognize and use relationships between and among polygons.
- Provide informal tessellation experiences.

Problem-solving skills pupils might use:

- Make a model.
- Guess and check.

Materials needed:

- One set of tangram pieces for each pupil (reproduced on tag or coverstock using the pattern on page 168).

Comments and suggestions:

- Pupils can complete this activity on their own or by working with a partner. Results are to be recorded by tracing the pieces used to cover the shapes on the worksheet.
- Pupils who complete the activity ahead of others can create other polygons or designs using the tangram pieces.

Answers:

Answers can vary. One way is shown below.

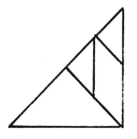 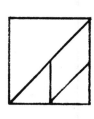 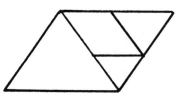

Use:

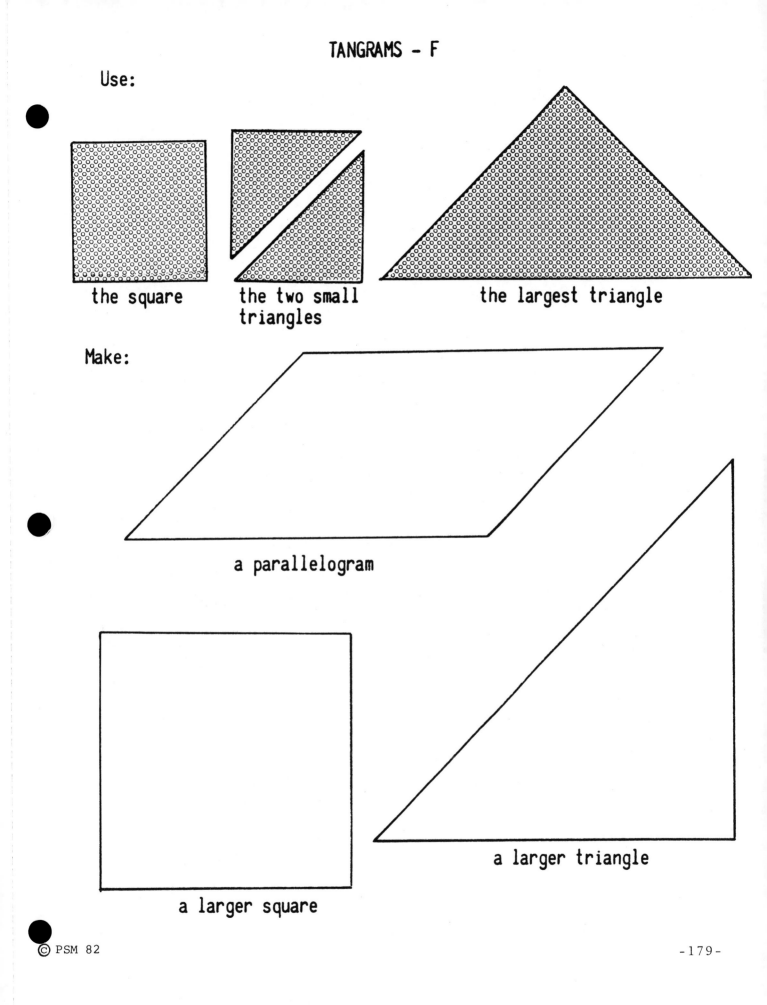

the square

the two small
triangles

the largest triangle

Make:

a parallelogram

a larger square

a larger triangle

Tangrams - F

Mathematics teaching objectives:

- Recognize polygons (square, triangle, parallelogram).
- Recognize and use relationships between and among polygons.
- Provide informal tessellation experiences.

Problem-solving skills pupils might use:

- Make a model.
- Guess and check.

Materials needed:

- One set of tangram pieces for each pupil (reproduced on tag or coverstock using the pattern on page 168).

Comments and suggestions:

- Pupils can complete this activity on their own or by working with a partner. Results are to be recorded by tracing the pieces used to cover the shapes on the worksheet.
- Pupils who complete the activity ahead of others can create other polygons or designs using the tangram pieces.

Answers:

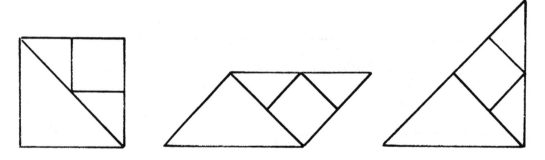

TANGRAMS - G

1. Use any four triangles. Cover each shape below.

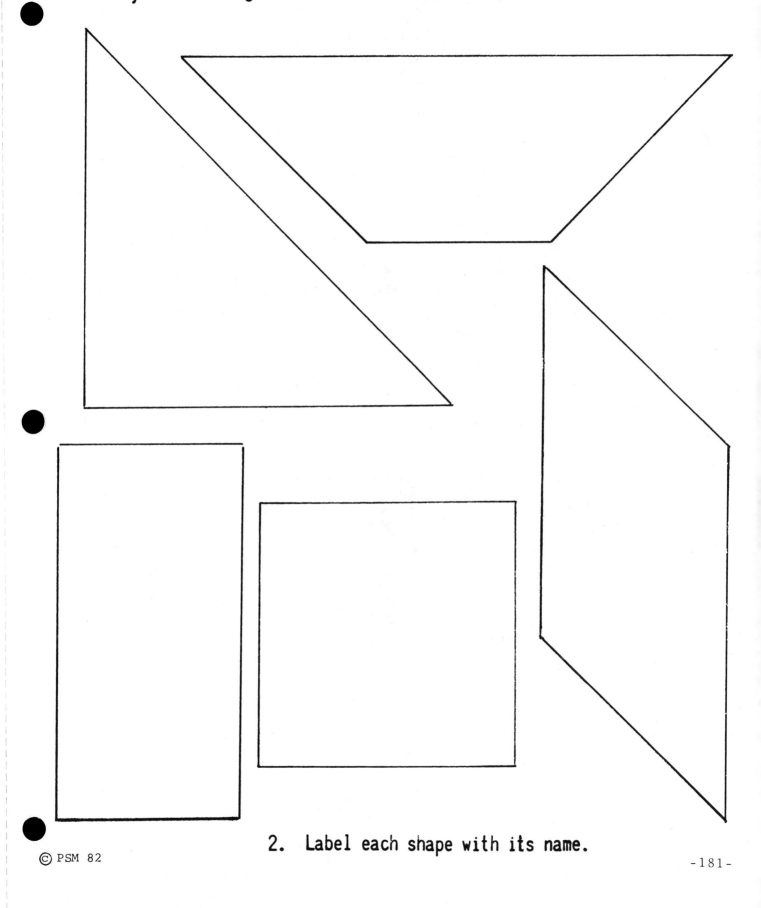

2. Label each shape with its name.

Mathematics teaching objectives:

- Recognize and name polygons (triangle, square, rectangle, trapezoid, parallelogram).
- Recognize and use relationships between and among polygons.
- Provide informal tessellation experiences.

Problem-solving skills pupils might use:

- Make a model.
- Guess and check.

Materials needed:

- One set of tangram pieces for each pupil (reproduced on tag or coverstock using the pattern on page 168).

Comments and suggestions:

- Pupils can complete this activity on their own or by working with a partner. Results are to be recorded by tracing the pieces used to cover the shapes on the worksheet.
- Pupils who complete the activity ahead of others can create other polygons or designs using the tangram pieces.
- A hint to use only one large triangle may be necessary.

Answers:

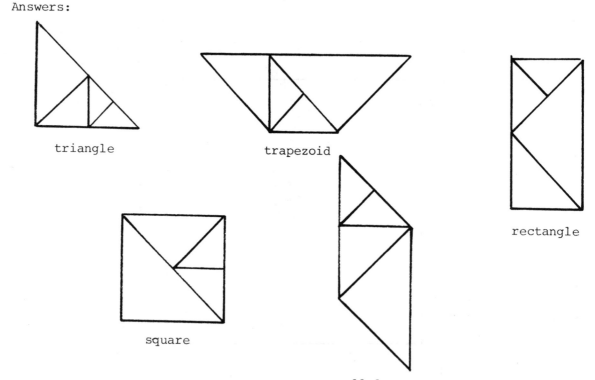

triangle

trapezoid

rectangle

square

parallelogram

IV. PATTERNS

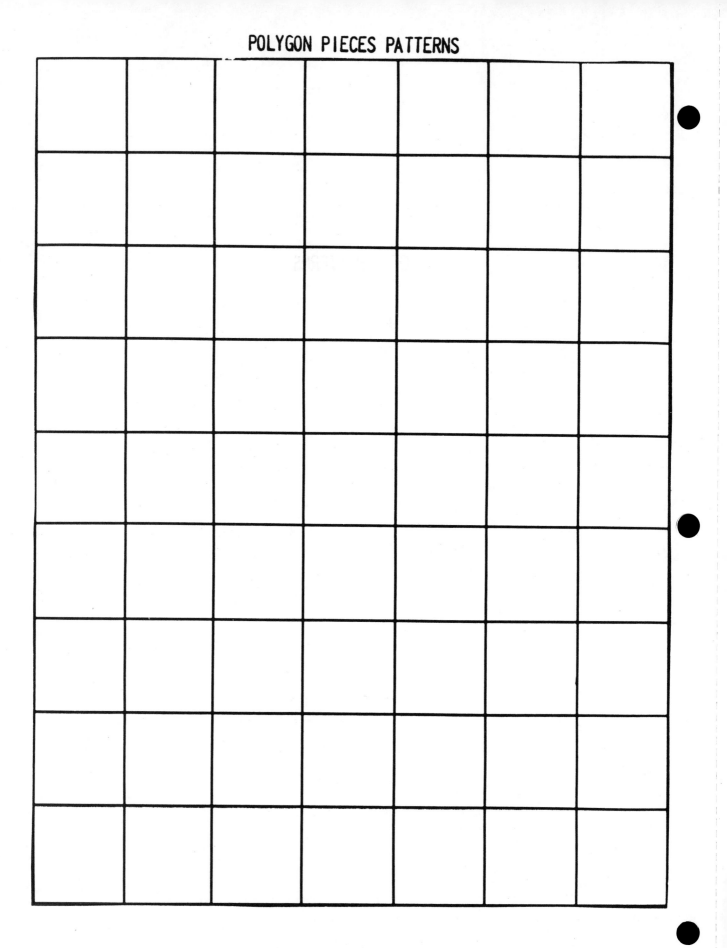

orange

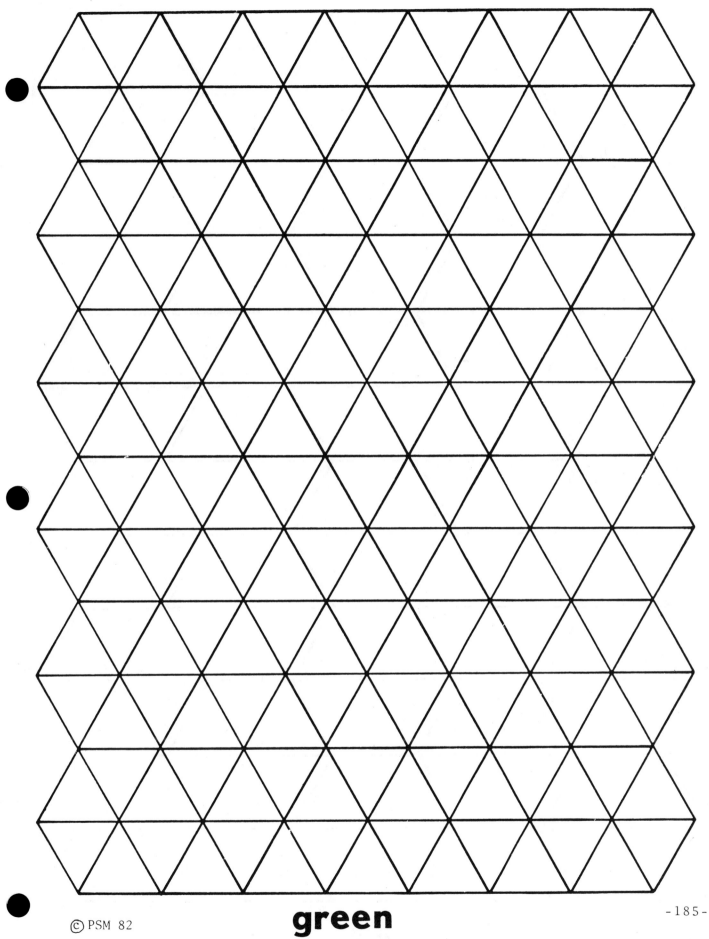

green

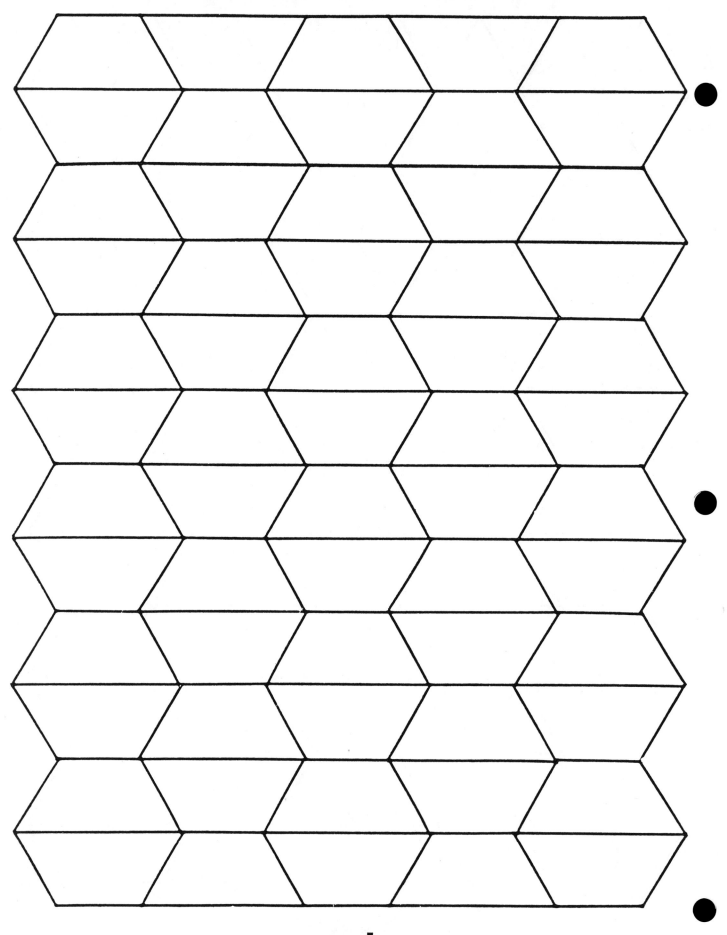

red

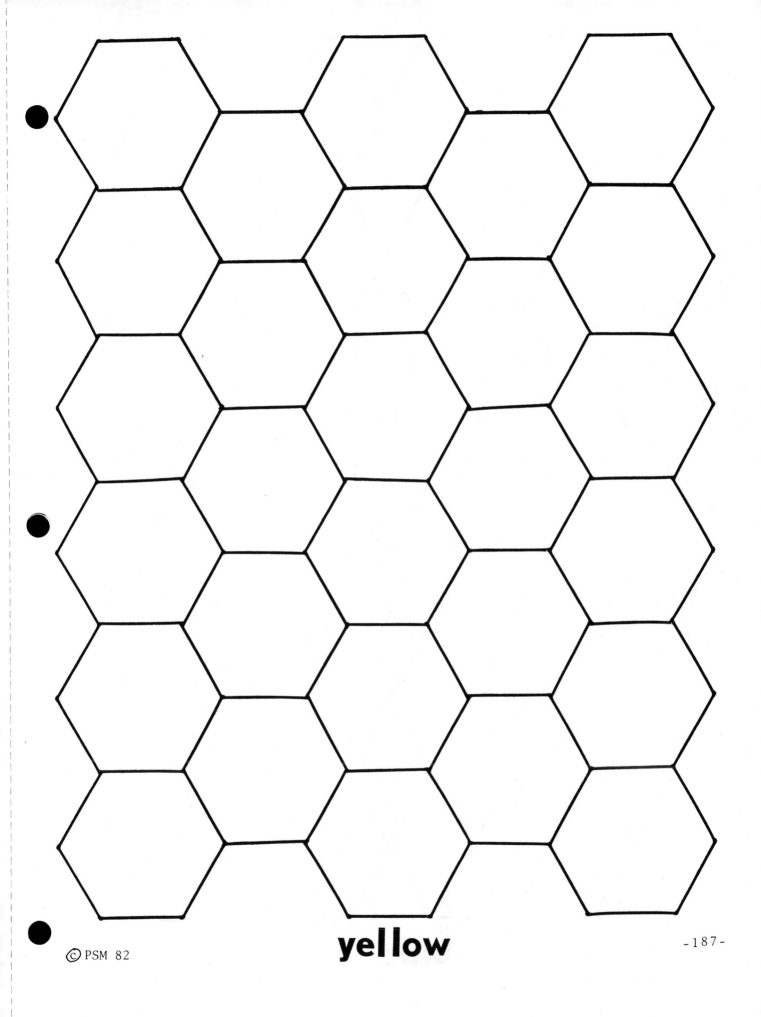

yellow

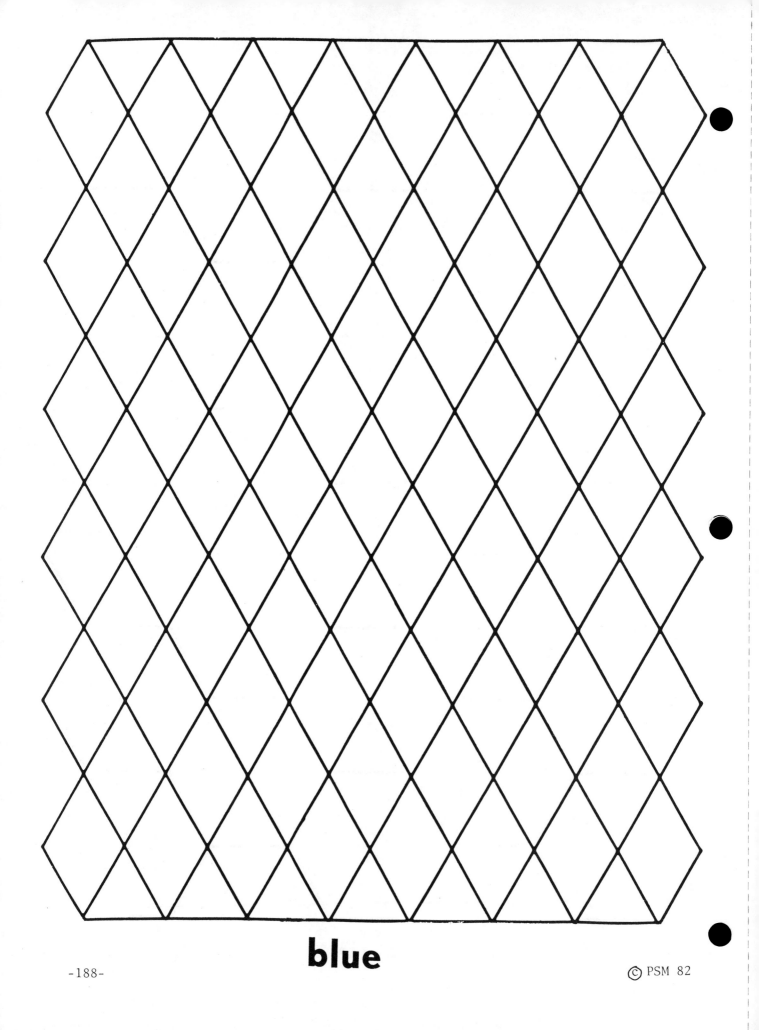

blue

PAPER CUT-UPS

Cover each shape below with <u>two</u> polygon pieces. Record.

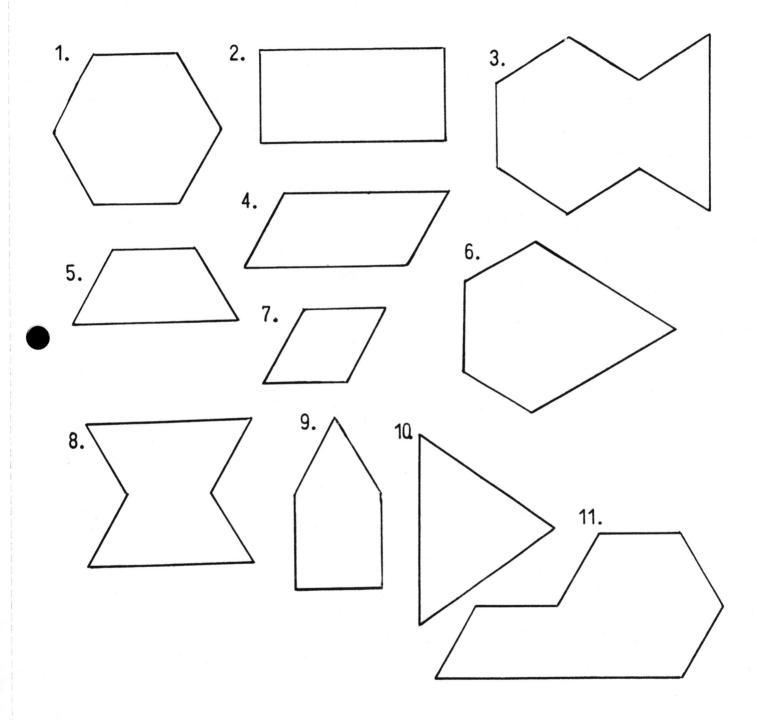

1.

2.

3.

4.

5.

6.

7.

8.

9.

10.

11.

© PSM 82

Paper Cut-Ups

Mathematics teaching objectives:

. Recognize and use relationships among polygons.

. Provide informal experiences with tessellations.

Problem-solving skills pupils _might_ use:

. Make a model.

. Guess and check.

Materials needed:

. Paper pieces (To make a <u>classroom</u> <u>set</u> of paper polygon pieces, reproduce the five pages of patterns on pages 184-188   on the colors of construction paper indicated. Make 10 copies of each page. Cut apart. [Pupils can do this.] Package pieces into enough sets for use in your classroom.)

. Crayons (optional)

. Actual sets of Pattern Blocks can be used. Pattern Blocks are available from several education supply outlets.

Comments and suggestions:

. Have pupils work in pairs. Pupils should <u>record</u> results by <u>tracing</u> the polygons used to cover the shapes on the worksheet and labeling the spaces with the color of the piece. Or, pupils can use crayons to color in the spaces. Pupils who complete the activity ahead of others can create their own designs and tessellations using the polygon pieces.

Answers:

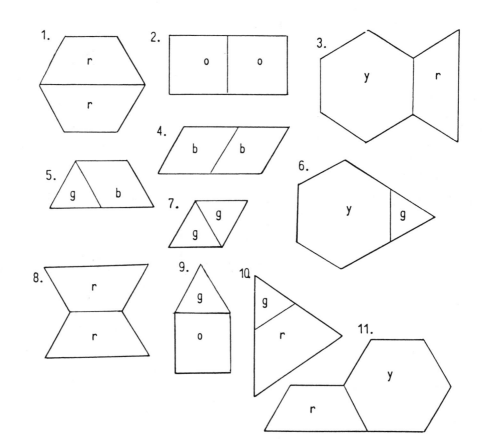

COVER WITH THREE

1. Cover each shape below with <u>3</u> polygon pieces. Record.

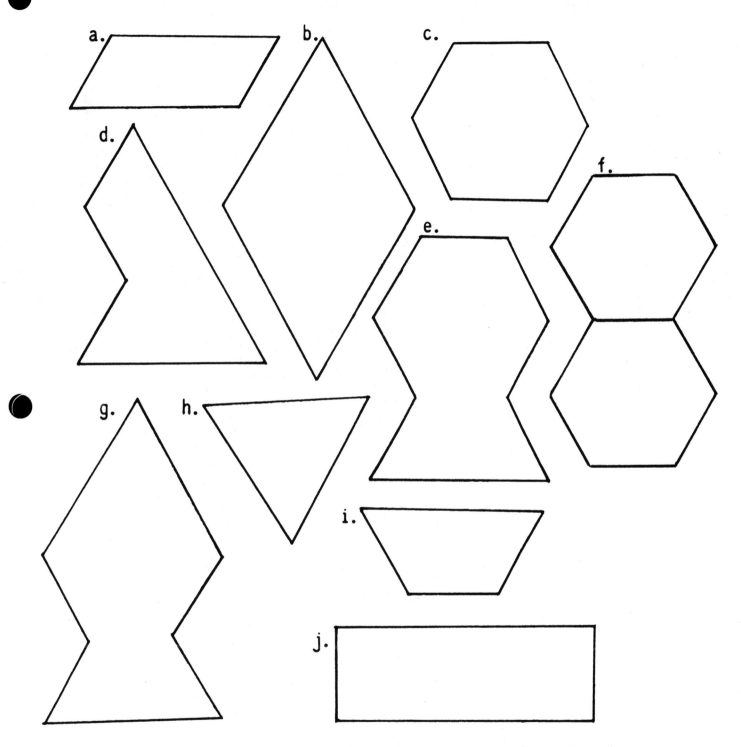

2. Find other shapes you can make with <u>3</u> pieces. Record each on the back of this paper.

Cover With Three

Mathematics teaching objectives:

. Recognize and use relationships among polygons.

. Provide informal experiences with tessellations.

Problem-solving skills pupils might use:

. Make a model.

. Guess and check.

Materials needed:

. Paper pieces (To make a classroom set of paper polygon pieces, reproduce
the five pages of patterns on pages 184-188   on the
colors of construction paper indicated. Make 10 copies of
each page. Cut apart. [Pupils can do this.] Package
pieces into enough sets for use in your classroom.)

. Crayons (optional)

. Actual sets of Pattern Blocks can be used. Pattern Blocks are available
from several education supply outlets.

Comments and suggestions:

. Have pupils work in pairs. Pupils should record results by tracing the
polygons used to cover the shapes on the worksheet and labeling the spaces
with the color of the piece. Or, pupils can use crayons to color in the
spaces. Pupils who complete the activity ahead of others can create their
own designs and tessellations using the polygon pieces.

Answers:

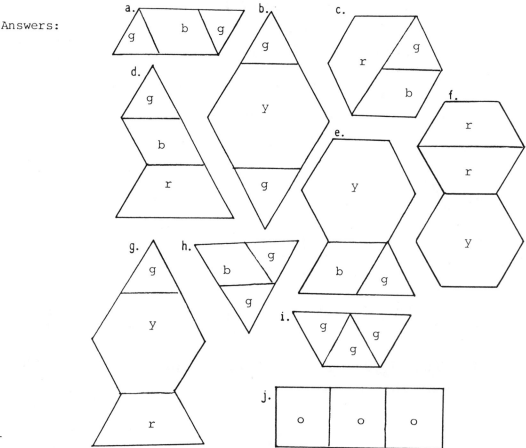

COVER WITH FOUR

Cover each shape with 4 polygon pieces.   Record.

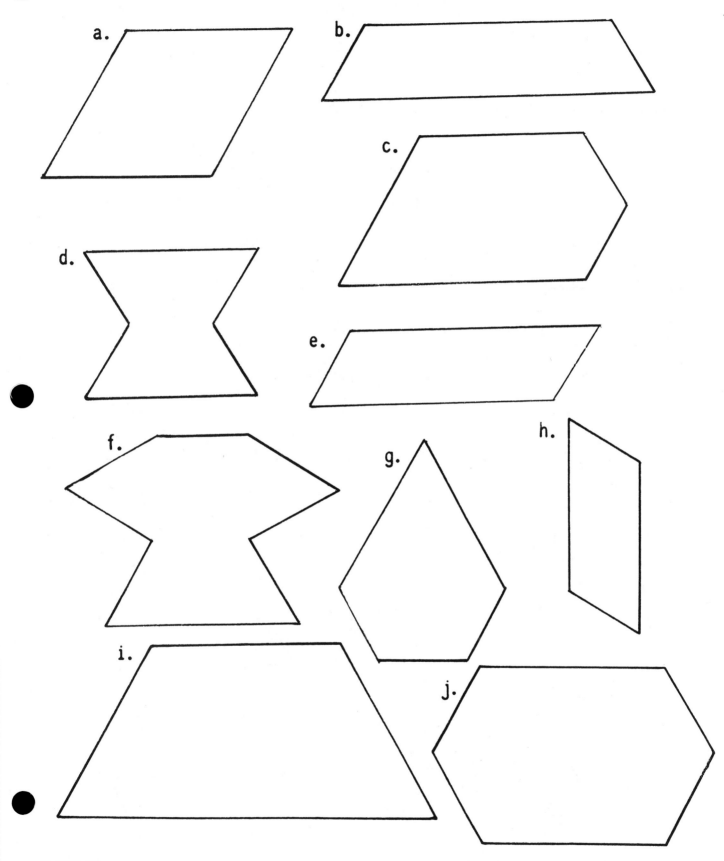

Cover With Four

Mathematics teaching objectives:

- Recognize and use relationships among polygons.
- Provide informal experiences with tessellations.

Problem-solving skills pupils might use:

- Make a model.
- Guess and check.

Materials needed:

- Paper pieces (To make a classroom set of paper polygon pieces, reproduce
  the five pages of patterns on pages 184-188   on the
  colors of construction paper indicated. Make 10 copies of
  each page. Cut apart. [Pupils can do this.] Package
  pieces into enough sets for use in your classroom.)

- Crayons (optional)

- Actual sets of Pattern Blocks can be used. Pattern Blocks are available
  from several education supply outlets.

Comments and suggestions:

- Have pupils work in pairs. Pupils should record results by tracing the
  polygons used to cover the shapes on the worksheet and labeling the spaces
  with the color of the piece. Or, pupils can use crayons to color in the
  spaces. Pupils who complete the activity ahead of others can create their
  own designs and tessellations using the polygon pieces.

Answers:

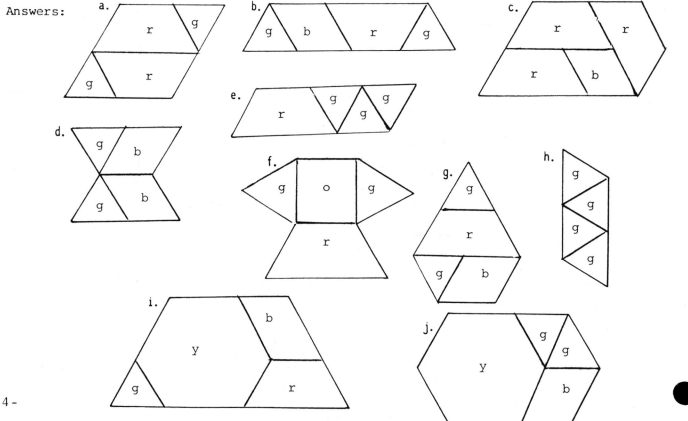

-194-

MAKE EACH DIFFERENT

Use polygon pieces. Cover each a <u>different</u> way. Record.

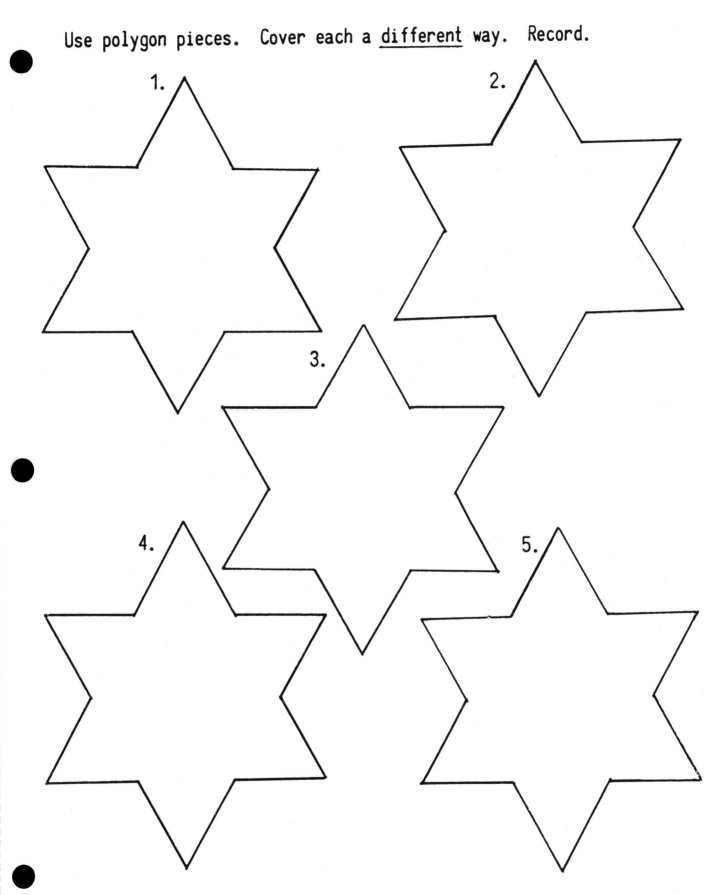

1.

2.

3.

4.

5.

Try to find still other ways. Record them on the back of this paper.

Make Each Different

Mathematics teaching objectives:

. Recognize and use relationships among polygons.

. Provide informal experiences with tessellations.

Problem-solving skills pupils might use:

. Make a model.

. Guess and check.

Materials needed:

. Paper pieces (To make a classroom set of paper polygon pieces, reproduce
the five pages of patterns on pages 184-188   on the
colors of construction paper indicated. Make 10 copies of
each page. Cut apart. [Pupils can do this.] Package
pieces into enough sets for use in your classroom.)

. Crayons (optional)

. Actual sets of Pattern Blocks can be used. Pattern Blocks are available
from several education supply outlets.

Comments and suggestions:

. Have pupils work in pairs. Pupils should record results by tracing the
polygons used to cover the shapes on the worksheet and labeling the spaces
with the color of the piece. Or, pupils can use crayons to color in the
spaces. Pupils who complete the activity ahead of others can create their
own designs and tessellations using the polygon pieces.

Answers:

Answers will vary.
Some are shown here.

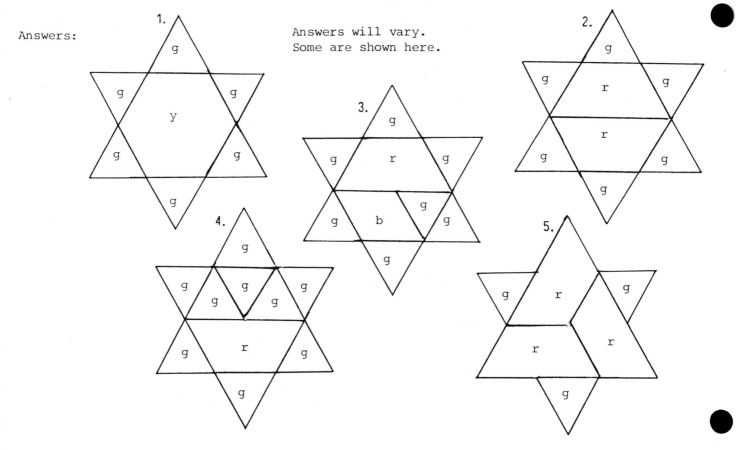

Use polygon pieces.
Cover the fish.
Make each one different.
Record.

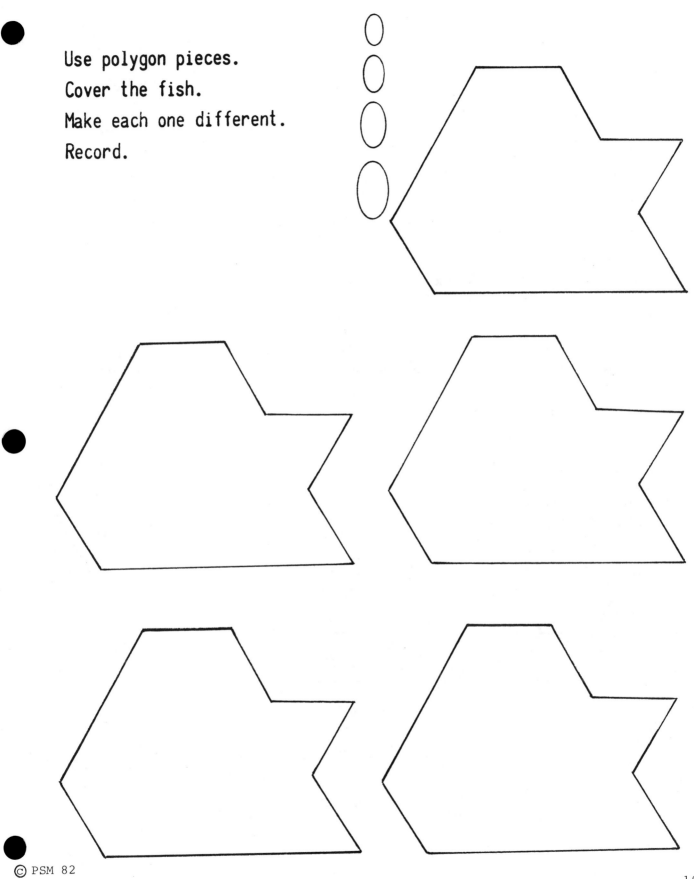

Mathematics teaching objectives:

- Recognize and use relationships among polygons.

- Provide informal experiences with tessellations.

Problem-solving skills pupils <u>might</u> use:

- Make a model.

- Guess and check.

Materials needed:

- Paper pieces (To make a <u>classroom</u> <u>set</u> of paper polygon pieces, reproduce the five pages of patterns on pages 184-188   on the colors of construction paper indicated. Make 10 copies of each page. Cut apart. [Pupils can do this.] Package pieces into enough sets for use in your classroom.)

- Crayons (optional)

- Actual sets of Pattern Blocks can be used. Pattern Blocks are available from several education supply outlets.

Comments and suggestions:

- Have pupils work in pairs. Pupils should <u>record</u> results by <u>tracing</u> the polygons used to cover the shapes on the worksheet and labeling the spaces with the color of the piece. Or, pupils can use crayons to color in the spaces. Pupils who complete the activity ahead of others can create their own designs and tessellations using the polygon pieces.

Answers:

Answers will vary.
Some correct answers
are shown here.

Use polygon pieces.
Cover the fish.
Make each one different.
Record.

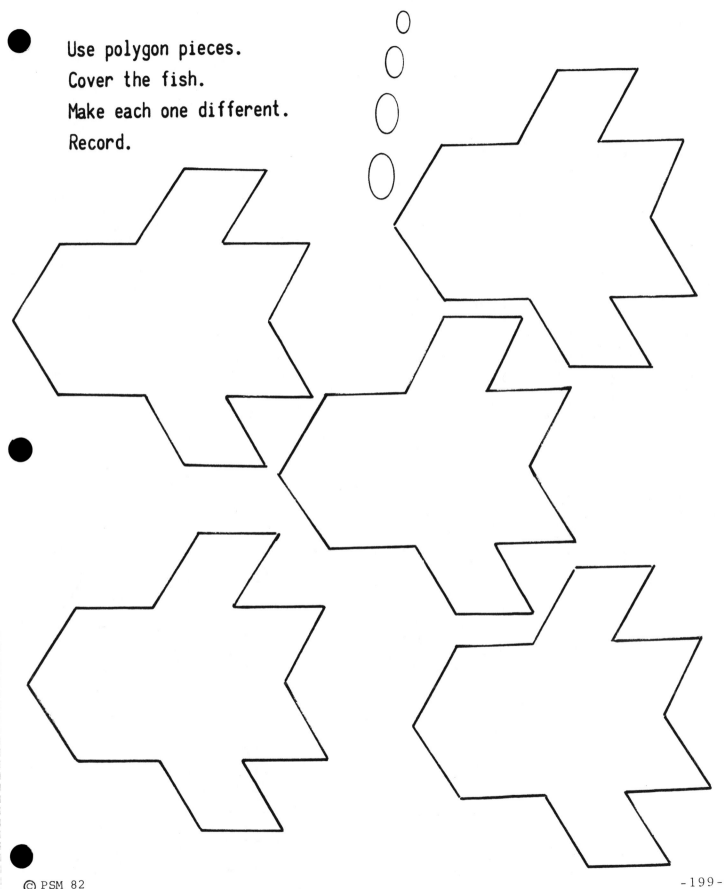

A Fishy Cover Up - B

Mathematics teaching objectives:

· Recognize and use relationships among polygons.

· Provide informal experiences with tessellations.

Problem-solving skills pupils might use:

· Make a model.

· Guess and check.

Materials needed:

· Paper pieces   (To make a classroom set of paper polygon pieces, reproduce the five pages of patterns on pages 184-188 on the colors of construction paper indicated. Make 10 copies of each page. Cut apart. [Pupils can do this.] Package pieces into enough sets for use in your classroom.)

· Crayons (optional)

· Actual sets of Pattern Blocks can be used. Pattern Blocks are available from several education supply outlets.

Comments and suggestions:

· Have pupils work in pairs. Pupils should record results by tracing the polygons used to cover the shapes on the worksheet and labeling the spaces with the color of the piece. Or, pupils can use crayons to color in the spaces. Pupils who complete the activity ahead of others can create their own designs and tessellations using the polygon pieces.

Answers:

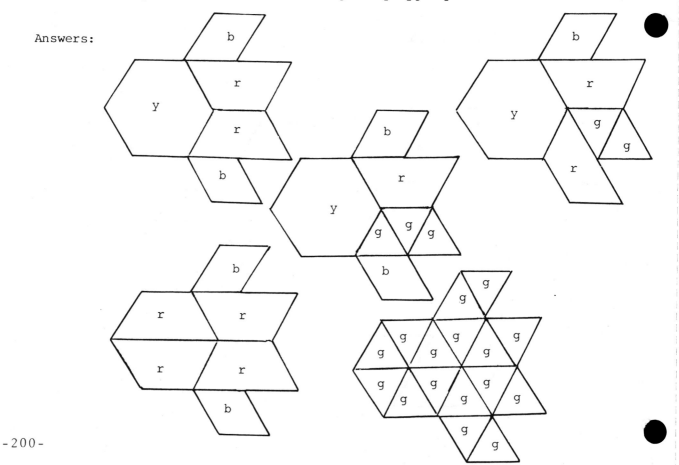

COVER THE TRIANGLES

Use polygon pieces. Cover the triangles. Make each <u>different</u>.
Follow the directions.

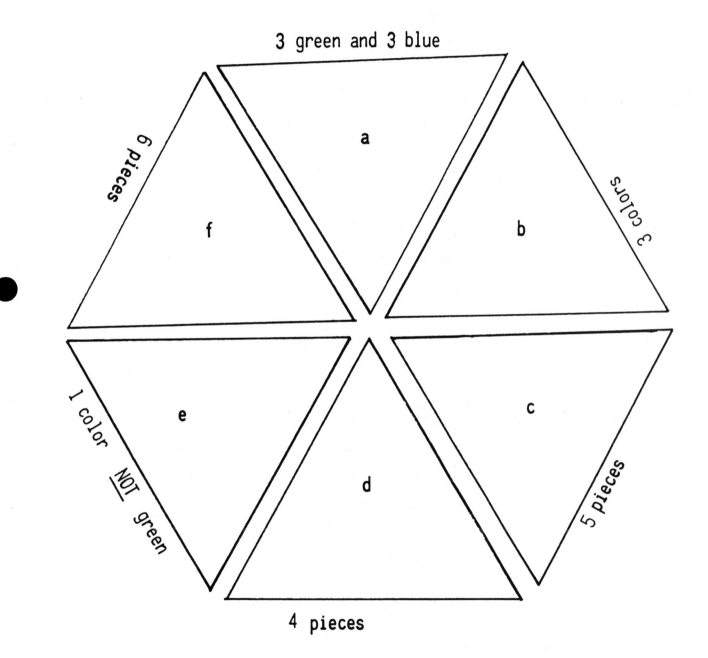

3 green and 3 blue

a

b

3 colors

f

6 pieces

1 color <u>NOT</u> green

e

d

c

5 pieces

4 pieces

Cover The Triangles

Mathematics teaching objectives:

- Recognize and use relationships among polygons.
- Provide informal experiences with tessellations.

Problem-solving skills pupils might use:

- Make a model.
- Guess and check.

Materials needed:

- Paper pieces (To make a classroom set of paper polygon pieces, reproduce the five pages of patterns on pages 184-188   on the colors of construction paper indicated. Make 10 copies of each page. Cut apart. [Pupils can do this.] Package pieces into enough sets for use in your classroom.)
- Crayons (optional)
- Actual sets of Pattern Blocks can be used. Pattern Blocks are available from several education supply outlets.

Comments and suggestions:

- Have pupils work in pairs. Pupils should record results by tracing the polygons used to cover the shapes on the worksheet and labeling the spaces with the color of the piece. Or, pupils can use crayons to color in the spaces. Pupils who complete the activity ahead of others can create their own designs and tessellations using the polygon pieces.

Answers: Answers will vary. One way is shown below.

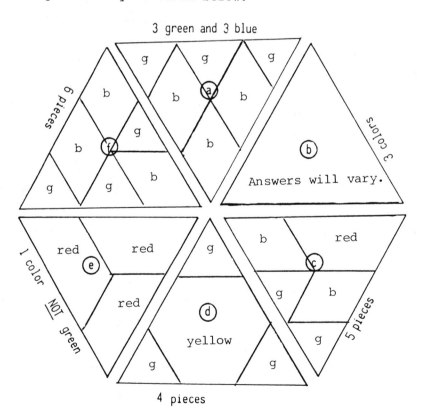

COVER WITH . . . .

Use polygon pieces. Follow the directions below. Cover each shape. Record.

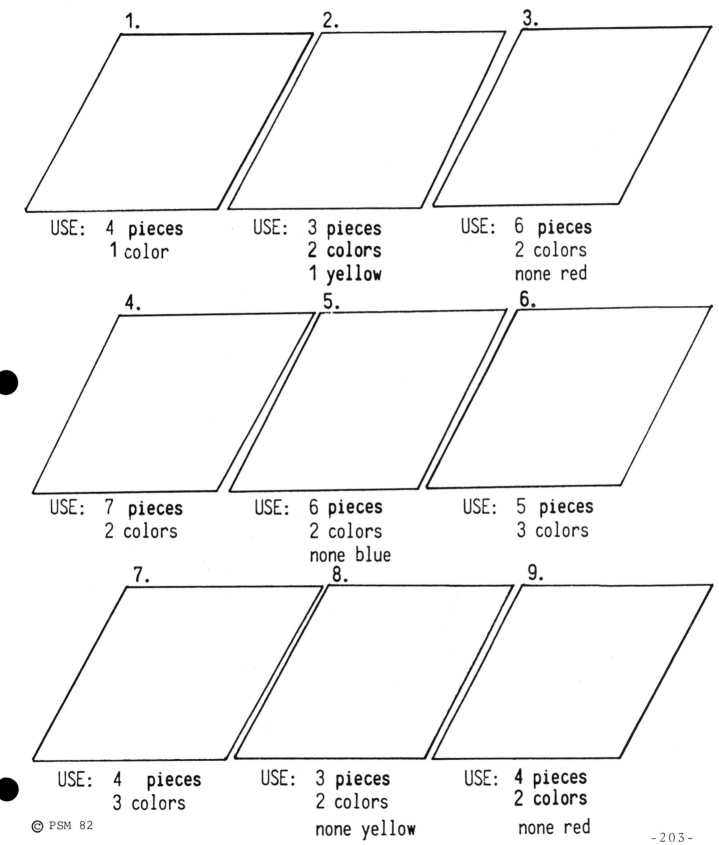

1.

USE: 4 **pieces**
      1 color

2.

USE: 3 **pieces**
      2 **colors**
      1 **yellow**

3.

USE: 6 **pieces**
      2 colors
      none red

4.

USE: 7 **pieces**
      2 colors

5.

USE: 6 **pieces**
      2 colors
      none blue

6.

USE: 5 **pieces**
      3 colors

7.

USE: 4 **pieces**
      3 colors

8.

USE: 3 **pieces**
      2 colors
      none yellow

9.

USE: 4 **pieces**
      2 **colors**
      none red

Cover With . . . .

Mathematics teaching objectives:

 . Recognize and use relationships among polygons.

 . Provide informal experiences with tessellations.

Problem-solving skills pupils might use:

 . Make a model.

 . Guess and check.

Materials needed:

 . Paper pieces (To make a classroom set of paper polygon pieces, reproduce
                 the five pages of patterns on pages 184-188   on the
                 colors of construction paper indicated. Make 10 copies of
                 each page. Cut apart. [Pupils can do this.] Package
                 pieces into enough sets for use in your classroom.)

 . Crayons (optional)

 . Actual sets of Pattern Blocks can be used. Pattern Blocks are available
   from several education supply outlets.

Comments and suggestions:

 . Have pupils work in pairs. Pupils should record results by tracing the
   polygons used to cover the shapes on the worksheet and labeling the spaces
   with the color of the piece. Or, pupils can use crayons to color in the
   spaces. Pupils who complete the activity ahead of others can create their
   own designs and tessellations using the polygon pieces.

Answers:

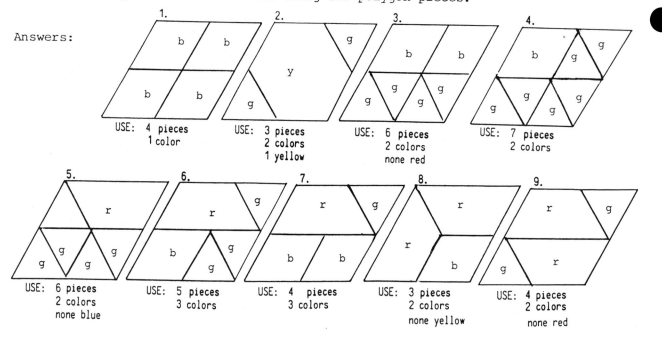

-204-

V. GEOMETRY

TILING SET PATTERN

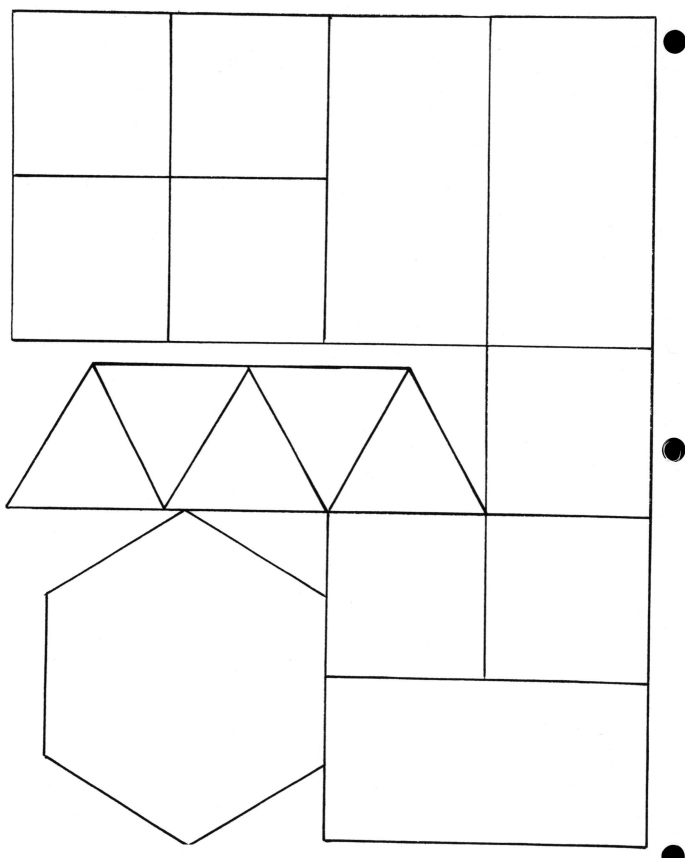

TILING SET PATTERN

TRIANGLES

1. These are triangles: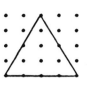

   Tell how they are alike: _____

   _____.

2. Use a geoboard and 3 rubber bands.

   Make other triangles. Make each of them different in some way.
   Record each below.

Triangles

Mathematics teaching objectives:

. Recognize triangles and properties of triangles.

Problem-solving skills pupils <u>might</u> use:

. Make a model.

Materials needed:

. One geoboard and three rubber bands (of various colors and sizes if possible) for each pair of pupils or for each individual pupil

Comments and suggestions:

. Discuss part 1 of the worksheet as a class.

. Pupils can complete the remainder of the page on their own or by working with a partner.

. Compare and discuss results when most pupils have completed the page.

Answers:

1. They all are polygons. They all have 3 sides and 3 corners. (Pupils will note <u>other</u> similarities.)

2. Answers will vary.

Note: A transparent geoboard for use on an overhead projector is useful for introducing and discussing geoboard activities.

RECTANGLES

These are rectangles.

These are <u>not</u> rectangles.

1. How are the rectangles alike? _____

_____

_____.

2. How are the other shapes different from the rectangles? _____

_____

_____.

3. Get a geoboard and 4 rubber bands. Make other rectangles. Record
   each below.

Rectangles

Mathematics teaching objectives:

. Recognize rectangles and their properties.

. Recognize that a square is one form of a rectangle.

Problem-solving skills pupils might use:

. Make a model.

. Sort and classify according to properties.

Materials needed:

. One geoboard for each pair of pupils or for each individual pupil

. Four rubber bands (of various colors and sizes if possible) for each pair of pupils.

Comments and suggestions:

. Discuss the two questions at the top of the worksheet as a class.

. After pupils have recorded their answers to those two questions, distribute geoboards and have pupils complete the activity working in pairs.

Answers:

1. They all are polygons. All have four sides. All have four corners. All have square corners. (Pupils will note other similarities, as well.)

2. They do not have all square corners. (Pupils will note other differences.)

3. Answers will vary.

Note: A transparent geoboard for use on an overhead projector is very helpful for introducing geoboard activities and for discussing and comparing results.

TILE PATTERNS

You will need . scissors
                       . four tiling set sheets (each a different color)

1. Cut out the shapes on the sheets.

    Count. How many . squares? ____
                      . long rectangles? ____
                      . triangles? ____
                      . hexagons? ____

2. Use just squares.
    Cover this sheet of paper.
    Do not leave gaps.
    Do not overlap pieces.

3. Use just long rectangles.
    Cover as much of this sheet as you can.

4. Use rectangles and squares.
    Cover this sheet.
    Show your teacher.

5. Use hexagons and triangles.
    Cover as much of this sheet as you can.
    Show your teacher.

EXTENSION

    Pick your own pieces.
    Cover a sheet of notebook paper.
    Glue or paste down your results.

<u>Tile</u> <u>Patterns</u>

Mathematics teaching objectives:

- Recognize polygons (square, rectangle, triangle, hexagon).
- Recognize relationships between and among polygons.
- Recognize and construct symmetrical designs using polygons.
- Recognize and construct tessellations using polygons.

Problem-solving skills pupils <u>might</u> use:

- Look for a pattern.
- Guess and check.
- Make a model.

Materials needed:

- One pair of scissors for each pupil or pair of pupils
- Four Tiling Set sheets (each a different color) for each pupil or pair of pupils   (For pattern, see page 206 .)
- Notebook paper or 9 x 12 newsprint (optional)
- Glue (optional)

Comments and suggestions:

- Before distributing materials or discussing the activity, have pupils look around the room for examples of shapes that go together without leaving space (tessellations). Some examples might include tiles on the floor or ceiling or brick or concrete block walls. Note that during today's math lesson, pupils will be getting a chance to create their own designs that go together without leaving spaces and without overlaps. Be certain pupils can identify the polygons used in the activity (square, rectangle, triangle, hexagon) and then distribute materials.
- If pupils work in pairs, you will need half as many materials.
- This activity is "checked" by circulating among pupils and noting their progress. You may want to make a class record sheet or list on which to place comments about each pupil's work as you move about the classroom. Some pupils will merely complete the activity; others will make more extensive and creative use of color, pattern, and symmetry. A checklist or comment sheet will enable you to note these individual differences.

Answers:

1. __28__ squares   __12__ long rectangles   __20__ triangles   __4__ hexagons

    Note: Squares are also rectangles. The "long rectangle" designation is intended to prevent pupils from counting the squares as rectangles. If pupils bring up this point, be sure to make this clarification.

2-5. Answers will vary. Make notes of particularly creative use of color, pattern, and symmetry.

UNDERCOVER CREATURES - A

Cut out the triangle units at the bottom of the page. Use them to cover the creatures below. Tell how many units cover each creature.

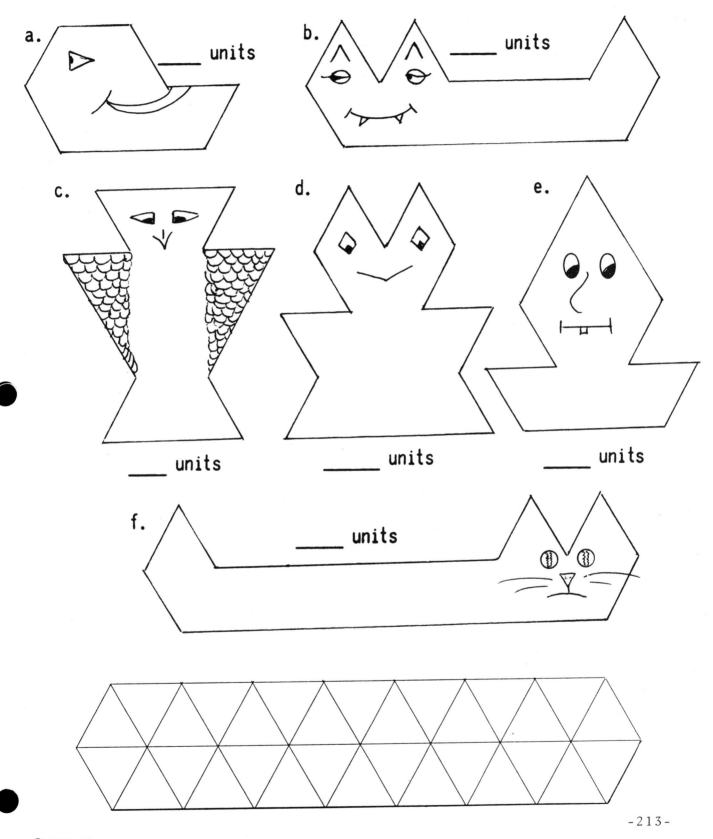

a. _____ units

b. _____ units

c. _____ units

d. _____ units

e. _____ units

f. _____ units

Undercover Creatures - A

Mathematics teaching objectives:

- Use area concepts.
- Determine area measurements of irregularly-shaped figures by covering with triangular units.

Problem-solving skills pupils might use:

- Make a model.

Materials needed:

- One pair of scissors for each pupil or pair of pupils.

Comments and suggestions:

- Discuss directions to the activity. Do one or two examples together, if needed. Have pupils complete the activity on their own.
- Discuss and compare results. Use the term "area" in discussing results, if appropriate.

Extension:

- Have pupils draw their own "Undercover Creatures" using a specified number of units of area.

Answers:

    a. 7 units

    b. 12 units

    c. 14 units

    d. 15 units

    e. 12 units

    f. 16 units

UNDERCOVER CREATURES - B

Cut out the square units at the bottom of the page. Use them to cover the creatures below. Tell how many units cover each creature.

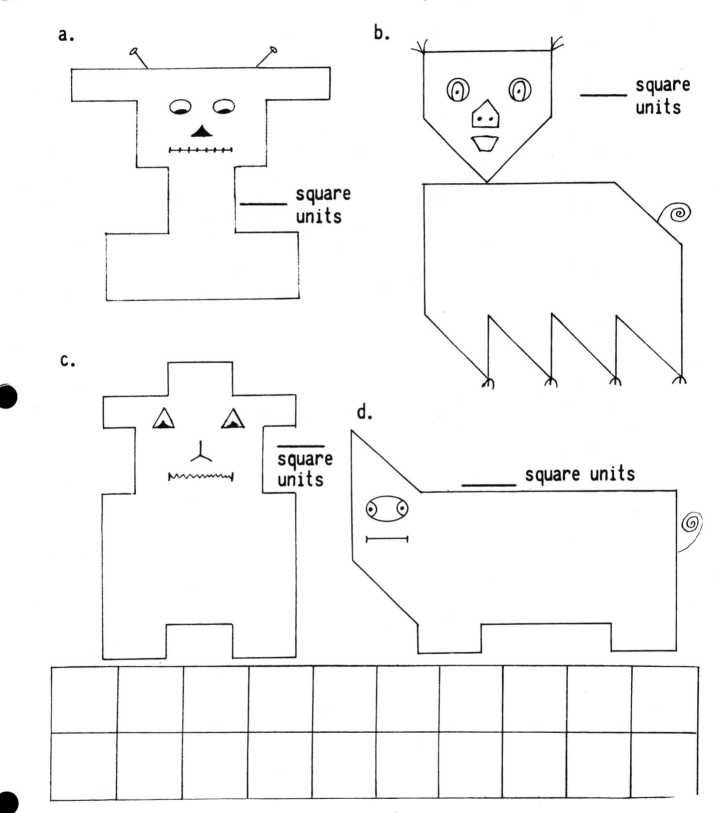

a.

_____ square units

b.

_____ square units

c.

_____ square units

d.

_____ square units

Undercover Creatures - <u>B</u>

Mathematics teaching objectives:

. Use area concepts.

. Determine area measurements of irregularly-shaped figures by covering with square units.

Problem-solving skills pupils <u>might</u> use:

. Make a model.

Materials needed:

. One pair of scissors for each pupil or pair of pupils.

Comments and suggestions:

. Discuss directions to the activity. Be certain pupils understand that they may need to fold some of their square units in half in order to measure the area accurately. If need be, do example 1 together and compare results.

. Have pupils finish the activity on their own. Compare and discuss results.

Extension:

. Have pupils draw their own "Undercover Creatures" using a <u>specified</u> number of units of area.

Answers:

a. 8 units

b. $12\frac{1}{2}$ units

c. 11 units

d. 11 units

TWO VIEWS

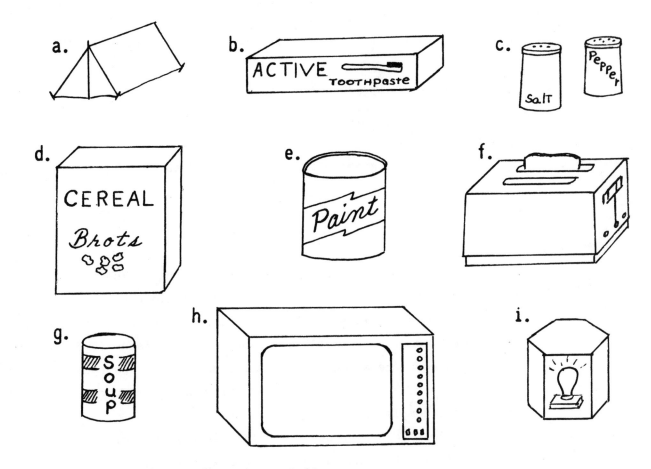

a. b. c.

d. CEREAL Brots egg

e. Paint

f.

g. SOUP

h.

i.

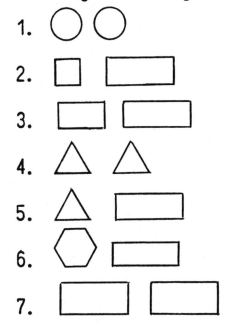

These are two different sides of the same object (or objects).

1. ◯ ◯

2. ▢ ▭

3. ▭ ▭

4. △ △

5. △ ▭

6. ⬡ ▭

7. ▭ ▭

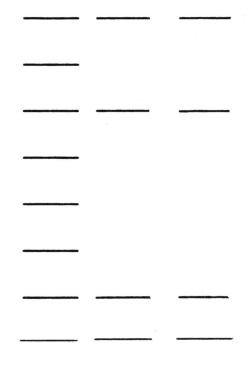

Which object(s)?

1. _____ _____ _____

2. _____

3. _____ _____ _____

4. _____

5. _____

6. _____

7. _____ _____ _____

_____ _____ _____

Two Views

Mathematics teaching objectives:

- Practice recognizing geometric shapes (2- and 3-dimensional) in real-world objects.
- Use visualization skills.

Problem-solving skills pupils <u>might</u> use:

- Look for a pattern.
- Search for printed materials for pertinent data.

Materials needed:

- None

Comments and suggestions:

- Note that the objects pictured at the top of the worksheet have the same basic shapes as some common three-dimensional figures. Explain that in the pictures we cannot see all faces (sides) of each object. Ask, "Which three pictured objects would have two circles as faces (sides)?" (c, e.g.) If needed, complete a few more examples as a class and then have pupils complete the worksheet on their own. Discuss and compare results when pupils have completed the activity.
- If time permits, make up other problems such as these, using items from the classroom. Present the clues verbally. Example: I am thinking of an item near the front of the room. It has 6 rectangular faces, is small, and is used many times a day. What is it? (chalkboard eraser)

Answers:

1. c, e, g
2. f
3. b, d, h
4. a
5. a
6. i
7. a, b, d, f, h, i

SUMS OF SHAPES

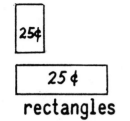 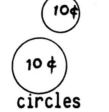 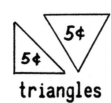 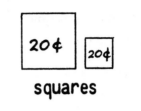 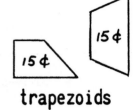

rectangles   circles   triangles   squares   trapezoids

1. This shape picture costs 60¢. Tell why.

2. Draw a car or truck that costs 75¢.

3. Draw a train that costs $1.00.

4. Draw shapes pictures that cost:

   a. 85¢

   b. $1.25

   c. $1.65

   d. $2.00

Sums Of Shapes

Mathematics teaching objectives:

- Recognize and use rectangles, circles, triangles, squares, and trapezoids.
- Solve addition (and subtraction) problems.
- Compute with money amounts.

Problem-solving skills pupils _might_ use:

- Make a drawing.
- Guess and check.

Materials needed:

- Crayons, colored pens or felt pens (optional)

Comments and suggestions:

- Review the names of the shapes at the top of the worksheet.
- Discuss part 1.
- Have pupils complete the remainder of the page on their own or by working with a partner.
- Share results as a class by posting results or by enlarging some specific ones and making a bulletin board display.

Answers:

1. 15¢ + 10¢ + 10¢ + 25¢ = 60¢, hence the picture is "worth" 60¢.

2-4. Answers will vary.

SQUARES - A

1. Cut out each of the four shapes at the bottom of this page.

2. Take shape A. Cut along the dotted line to make two pieces.

   Use the two pieces to cover the square.

3. Take shape B. Cut it into two pieces. Make a square.

4. Take shape C. Make a square.

5. Take shape D. Make <u>one straight cut</u>. Rearrange the two pieces to cover the square.

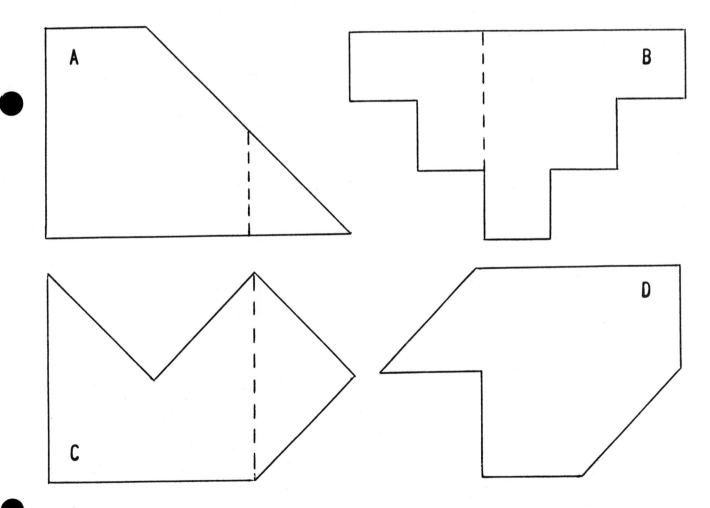

Show your completed squares to your teacher.

© PSM 82

Mathematics teaching objectives:

- Recognize squares and properties of squares.
- Use visualization skills to construct squares.

Problem-solving skills pupils <u>might</u> use:

- Make a drawing, diagram, or model.
- Guess and check.

Materials needed:

- One pair of scissors for each pupil (or pair of pupils)
- Extra copies of worksheet
- Straight edges for pupils who wish to use them

Comments and suggestions:

- Complete parts 1 and 2 as a class activity.
- Have pupils complete the remainder of the page on their own, or by working with a partner.
- Check pupils' completed results individually.

Answers:

A

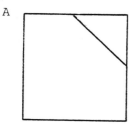

B

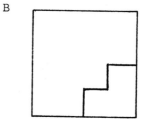

C

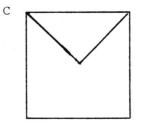

D

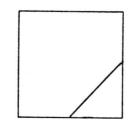

SQUARES - B

Cut out the shapes below.
● Set aside the shapes.

For each shape,

. make one straight cut.

. rearrange the two pieces to cover the square.

Show your four completed squares to your teacher.

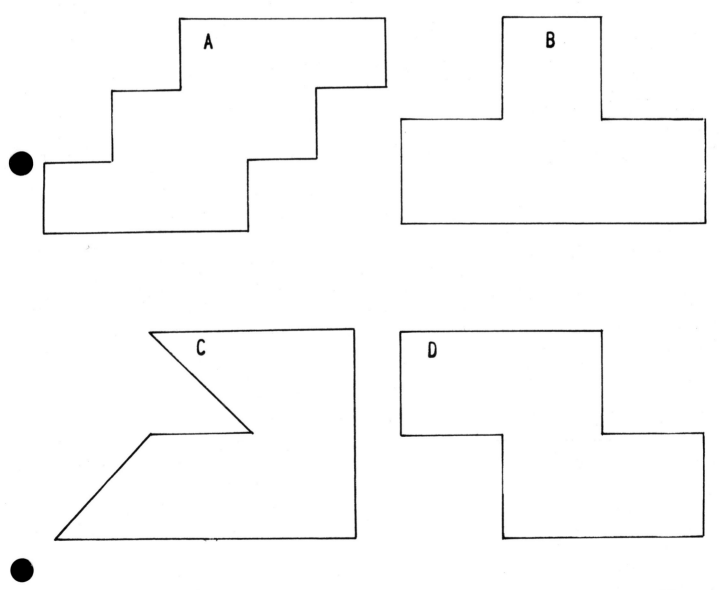

A

B

C

D

Squares - <u>B</u>

Mathematics teaching objectives:

    . Recognize squares and properties of squares.

    . Use visualization skills to construct squares.

Problem-solving skills pupils <u>might</u> use:

    . Make a drawing, diagram, or model.

    . Guess and check.

Materials needed:

    . One pair of scissors for each pupil (or pair of pupils)

    . Extra copies of the worksheet

    . Straight edges for pupils who wish to use them

Comments and suggestions:

    . Pupils can complete this activity on their own or by working with a partner.

    . Check pupils' results individually as they complete the assignment.

    . Some pupils will make errors and need an additional worksheet. Have extra copies available for such pupils.

Answers:

Cut on the dotted lines.

A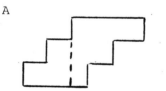

B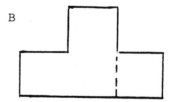

C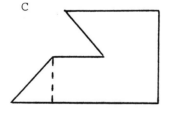

D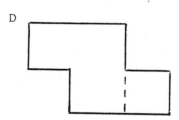

SQUARES - C

For each shape below,
- . make one straight cut.
- . rearrange the two pieces to make a square.

Show your completed squares to your teacher.

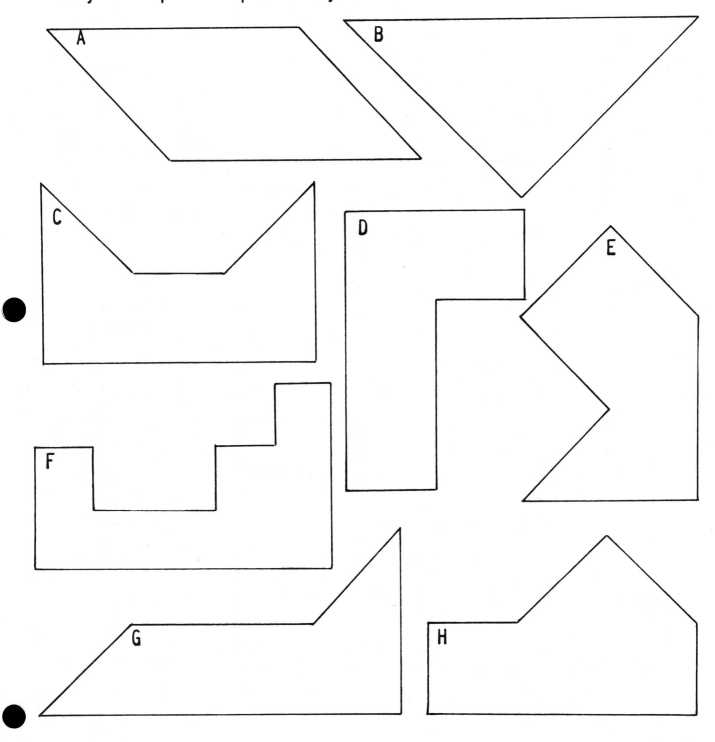

Squares - C

Mathematics teaching objectives:

. Recognize squares and properties of squares.

. Use visualization skills to construct squares.

Problem-solving skills pupils might use:

. Make a drawing, diagram, or model.

. Guess and check.

Materials needed:

. One pair of scissors for each pupil (or pair of pupils)

. Extra copies of the worksheet.

. Straight edges for pupils who wish to use them

Comments and suggestions:

. This is a more difficult activity than Squares - A and Squares - B.
  Allow plenty of time for pupils to complete the activity.

. Circulate among pupils to provide encouragement and assistance, if
  needed. Suggest pupils work with partners or in small groups.

. Have extra copies of the worksheet available for pupils who make errors.

Answers:

Cut on the dotted lines.

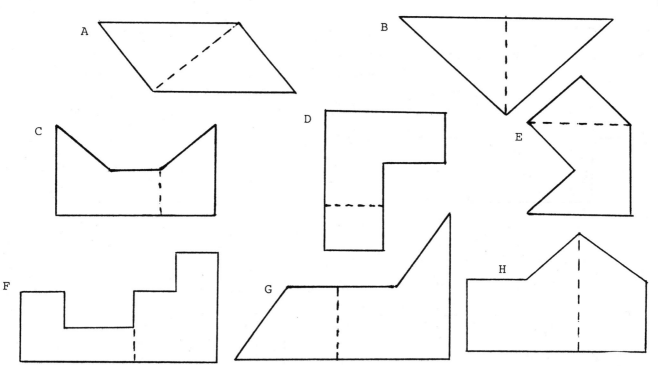

VI. CHALLENGE PROBLEMS

SHAPES SHEET PATTERN

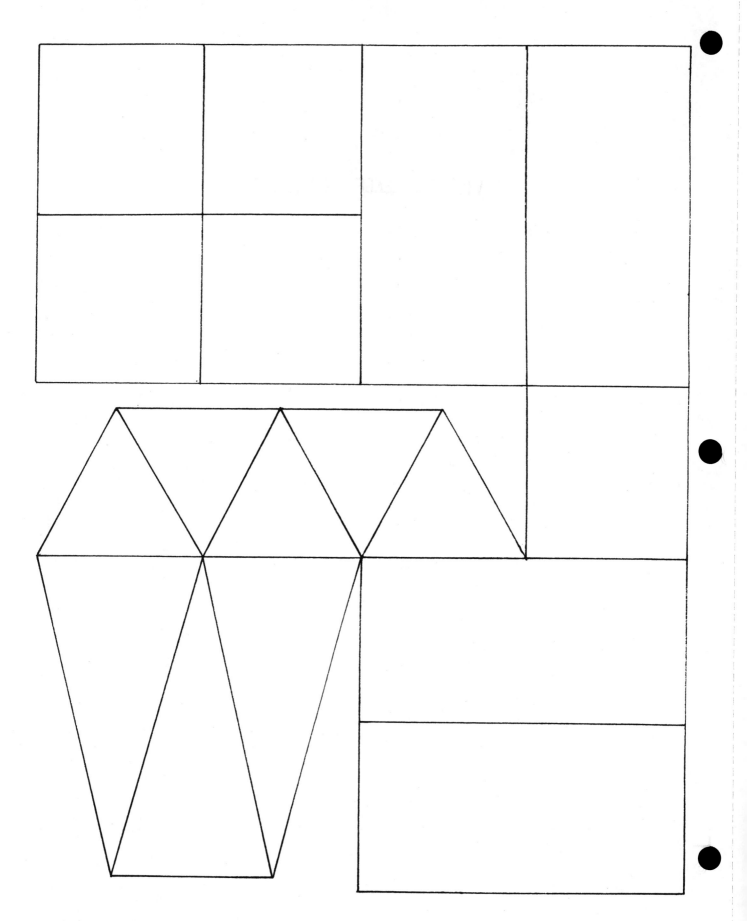

ADDITION CUT-UPS – A

Cut out the numbers 0 to 9 from the bottom of the page. Use all pieces.
Place them in the spaces below. Make each addition problem correct.
Record your findings.

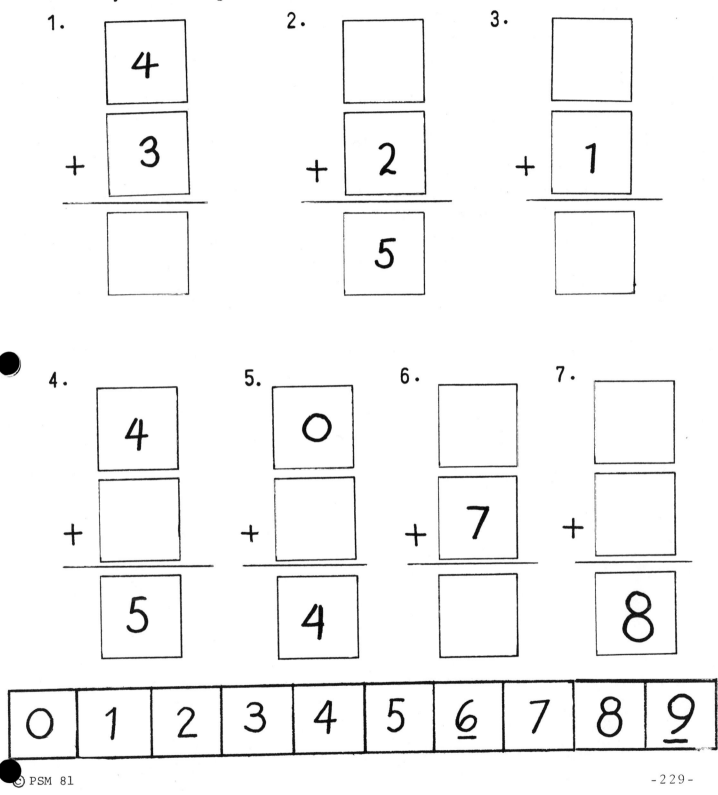

1.
  4
+ 3
___

2.
  [ ]
+ 2
___
  5

3.
  [ ]
+ 1
___
  [ ]

4.
  4
+ [ ]
___
  5

5.
  0
+ [ ]
___
  4

6.
  [ ]
+ 7
___
  [ ]

7.
  [ ]
+ [ ]
___
  8

0 1 2 3 4 5 6 7 8 9

Addition Cut-Ups - A

Mathematics teaching objectives:

- Practice addition facts.
- Find missing addends.
- Use addition/subtraction relationships.

Problem-solving skills pupils might use:

- Guess and check.
- Work backwards.
- Eliminate possibilities.

Materials needed:

- One pair of scissors for each pupil

Comments and suggestions:

- Be certain pupils understand the general directions. Then ask them to complete the page on their own.
- Pupils who are have difficulty may be encouraged to find and solve first those problems that have only one possible answer (i.e., 1, 2, 4, 5).

Answers:

1.   4
   + 3
     7
	2. 3
	   + 2
	     5
		3. 5
		   + 1
		     6

1.
$$\begin{array}{r} 4 \\ +\ 3 \\ \hline 7 \end{array}$$

2.
$$\begin{array}{r} 3 \\ +\ 2 \\ \hline 5 \end{array}$$

3.
$$\begin{array}{r} 5 \\ +\ 1 \\ \hline 6 \end{array}$$

4.
$$\begin{array}{r} 4 \\ +\ 1 \\ \hline 5 \end{array}$$

5.
$$\begin{array}{r} 0 \\ +\ 4 \\ \hline 4 \end{array}$$

6.
$$\begin{array}{r} 2 \\ +\ 7 \\ \hline 9 \end{array}$$

7.
$$\begin{array}{r} 8 \\ +\ 0 \\ \hline 8 \end{array}$$

ADDITION CUT-UPS - B

Cut out the numbers 0 to 9 from the bottom of the page.
Place them in the spaces below. All pieces must be used.
Make each addition problem correct. Record your findings.

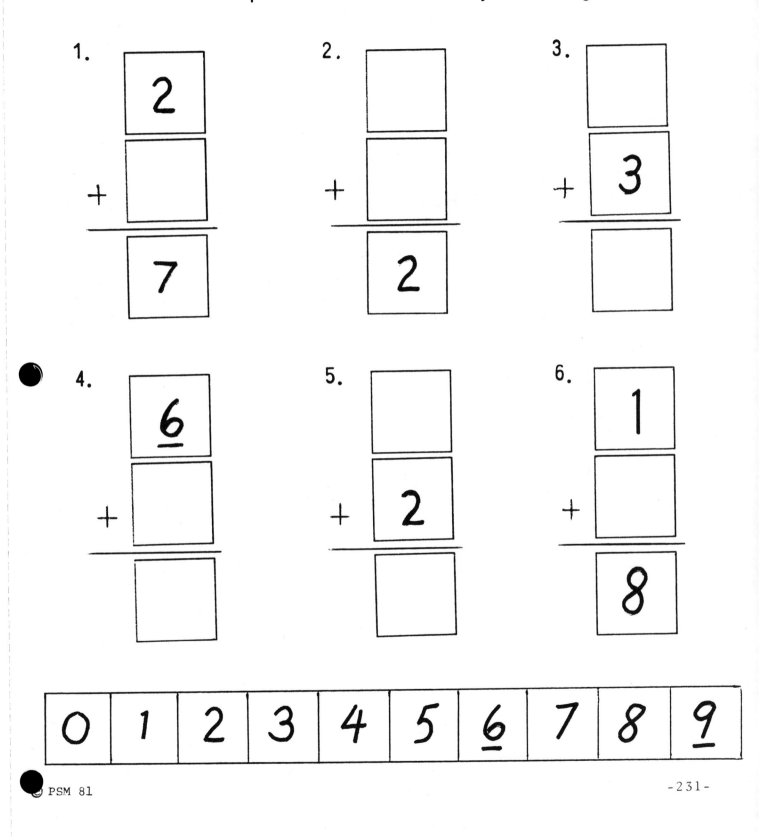

1.
```
   2
 +
 ───
   7
```

2.
```
 +
 ───
   2
```

3.
```
 + 3
 ───
```

4.
```
   6
 +
 ───
```

5.
```
 + 2
 ───
```

6.
```
   1
 +
 ───
   8
```

0	1	2	3	4	5	6	7	8	9

Addition Cut-Ups - B

Mathematics teaching objectives:

- Practice addition facts.
- Find missing addends.
- Use addition/subtraction relationships.

Problem-solving skills pupils might use:

- Guess and check.
- Work backwards.
- Eliminate possibilities.

Materials needed:

- One pair of scissors for each pupil

Comments and suggestions:

- Be certain pupils understand the general directions. Then ask them to complete the page on their own.

- Pupils who are having difficulty may be encouraged to find and solve first those problems that have only one possible answer (i.e., 1, 2, and 6).

Answers:

1. $\begin{array}{r} 2 \\ + 5 \\ \hline 7 \end{array}$	2. $\begin{array}{r} 0 \\ + 2 \\ \hline 2 \end{array}$ or $\begin{array}{r} 2 \\ + 0 \\ \hline 2 \end{array}$	3. $\begin{array}{r} 1 \\ + 3 \\ \hline 4 \end{array}$
4. $\begin{array}{r} 6 \\ + 3 \\ \hline 9 \end{array}$	5. $\begin{array}{r} 6 \\ + 2 \\ \hline 8 \end{array}$	6. $\begin{array}{r} 1 \\ + 7 \\ \hline 8 \end{array}$

ADDITION CUT-UPS – C

Cut out the numbers 0 to 9 from the bottom of the page. Use all pieces.
Place them in the spaces below. Make each addition problem correct.
Record your findings.

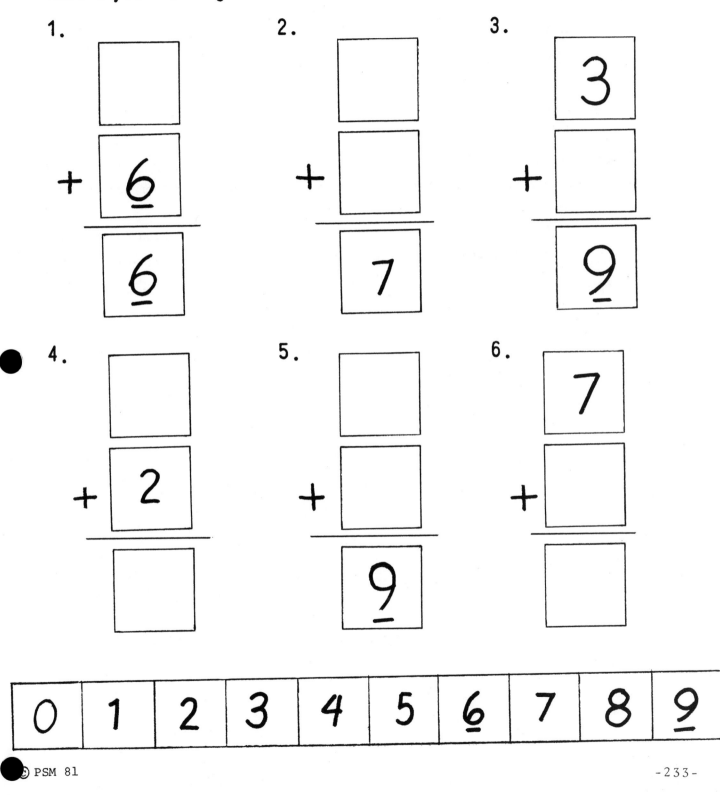

1.
    ☐
+   6
────
    6

2.
    ☐
+   ☐
────
    7

3.
    3
+   ☐
────
    9

4.
    ☐
+   2
────
    ☐

5.
    ☐
+   ☐
────
    9

6.
    7
+   ☐
────
    ☐

| 0 | 1 | 2 | 3 | 4 | 5 | 6 | 7 | 8 | 9 |

Addition Cut-Ups - C

Mathematics teaching objectives:

. Practice addition facts.

. Find missing addends.

. Use addition/subtraction relationships.

Problem-solving skills pupils might use:

. Guess and check.

. Work backwards.

. Eliminate possibilities.

Materials needed:

. One pair of scissors for each pupil

Comments and suggestions:

. Be certain pupils understand the general directions. Then ask them
to complete the page on their own.

. Pupils who are having difficulty may be encouraged to find and solve
first those problems that have only one possible answer, i.e., 1 and 3.

Answers:

1.
$$\begin{array}{r} 0 \\ +\ 6 \\ \hline 6 \end{array}$$

2.
$$\begin{array}{r} 3 \\ +\ 4 \\ \hline 7 \end{array}$$ or $$\begin{array}{r} 4 \\ +\ 3 \\ \hline 7 \end{array}$$

3.
$$\begin{array}{r} 3 \\ +\ 6 \\ \hline 9 \end{array}$$

4.
$$\begin{array}{r} 5 \\ +\ 2 \\ \hline 7 \end{array}$$

5.
$$\begin{array}{r} 8 \\ +\ 1 \\ \hline 9 \end{array}$$ or $$\begin{array}{r} 1 \\ +\ 8 \\ \hline 9 \end{array}$$

6.
$$\begin{array}{r} 7 \\ +\ 2 \\ \hline 9 \end{array}$$

SUBTRACTION CUT-UPS - A

Cut out the numbers 0 to 9 from the bottom of the page. Use all pieces. Place them in the spaces below. Make each subtraction problem correct. Record your findings.

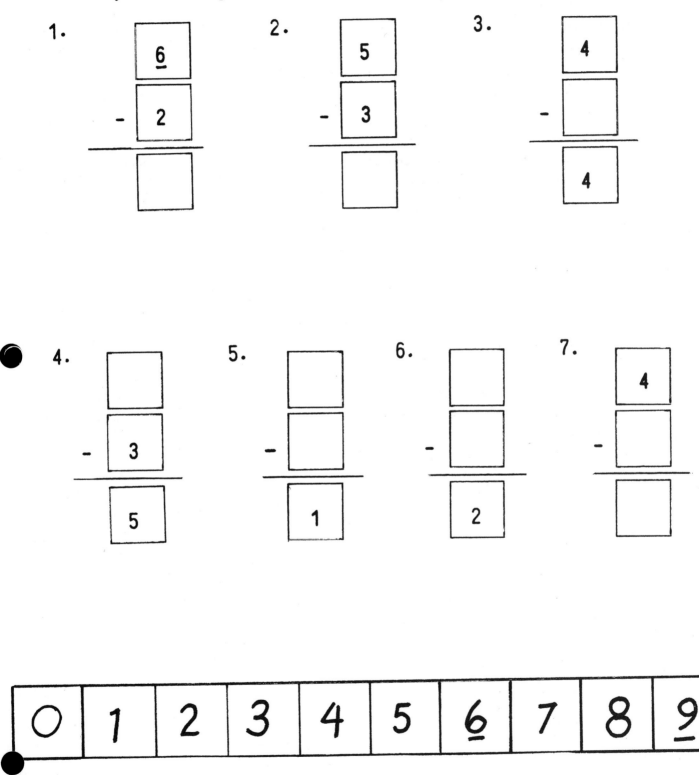

1.
```
    6
  - 2
  ___
```

2.
```
    5
  - 3
  ___
```

3.
```
    4
  - □
  ___
    4
```

4.
```
    □
  - 3
  ___
    5
```

5.
```
    □
  - □
  ___
    1
```

6.
```
    □
  - □
  ___
    2
```

7.
```
    4
  - □
  ___
    □
```

| O | 1 | 2 | 3 | 4 | 5 | 6 | 7 | 8 | 9 |

Subtraction Cut-Ups - A

Mathematics teaching objectives:

- Practice subtraction facts.
- Use addition/subtraction relationships.

Problem-solving skills pupils might use:

- Guess and check.
- Work backwards.
- Eliminate possibilities.

Materials needed:

- One pair of scissors for each pupil

Comments and suggestions:

- Be certain pupils understand the general directions. Then ask them
  to complete the page on their own.
- Pupils who are having difficulty may be encouraged to find and solve
  first those problems that have only one possible answer (i.e., 1, 2, 3,
  and 4).

Answers:

1.
$$\begin{array}{r} 6 \\ -\ 2 \\ \hline 4 \end{array}$$

2.
$$\begin{array}{r} 5 \\ -\ 3 \\ \hline 2 \end{array}$$

3.
$$\begin{array}{r} 4 \\ -\ 0 \\ \hline 4 \end{array}$$

4.
$$\begin{array}{r} 8 \\ -\ 3 \\ \hline 5 \end{array}$$

5.
$$\begin{array}{r} 6 \\ -\ 5 \\ \hline 1 \end{array}$$

6.
$$\begin{array}{r} 7 \\ -\ 5 \\ \hline 2 \end{array}$$

7.
$$\begin{array}{r} 4 \\ -\ 3 \\ \hline 1 \end{array} \quad or \quad \begin{array}{r} 4 \\ -\ 1 \\ \hline 3 \end{array}$$

SUBTRACTION CUT-UPS - B

Cut out the numbers 0 to 9 from the bottom of the page. Use all pieces. Place them in the spaces below. Make each subtraction problem correct. Record your findings.

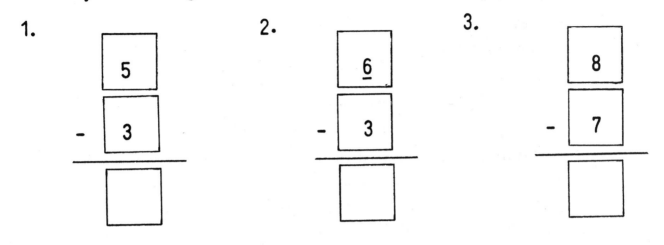

1.
```
    5
  -  3
  ─────
```

2.
```
    6
  -  3
  ─────
```

3.
```
    8
  -  7
  ─────
```

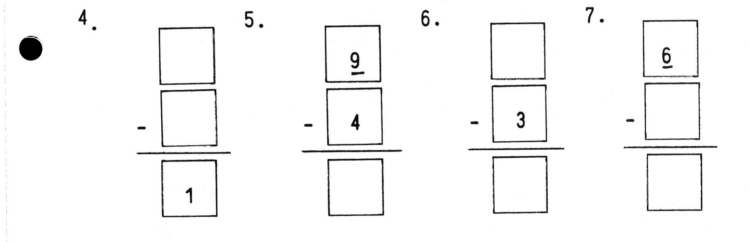

4.
```
  -
  ─────
    1
```

5.
```
    9
  -  4
  ─────
```

6.
```
  -  3
  ─────
```

7.
```
    6
  -
  ─────
```

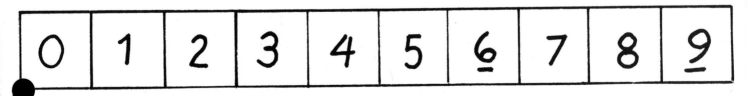

0 1 2 3 4 5 6 7 8 9

Subtraction Cut-Ups - B

Mathematics teaching objectives:

- Practice subtraction facts.
- Use addition/subtraction relationships.

Problem-solving skills pupils might use:

- Guess and check.
- Work backwards.
- Eliminate possibilities.

Materials needed:

- One pair of scissors for each pupil

Comments and suggestions:

- Be certain pupils understand the general directions. Then ask them to complete the page on their own.
- Pupils who are having difficulty may be encouraged to find and solve first those problems that have only one possible answer, i.e., 1, 2, 3, and 5.

Answers:

1.
$$\begin{array}{r} 5 \\ -\ 3 \\ \hline 2 \end{array}$$

2.
$$\begin{array}{r} 6 \\ -\ 3 \\ \hline 3 \end{array}$$

3.
$$\begin{array}{r} 8 \\ -\ 7 \\ \hline 1 \end{array}$$

4.
$$\begin{array}{r} 9 \\ -\ 8 \\ \hline 1 \end{array}$$

5.
$$\begin{array}{r} 9 \\ -\ 4 \\ \hline 5 \end{array}$$

6.
$$\begin{array}{r} 7 \\ -\ 3 \\ \hline 4 \end{array}$$

7.
$$\begin{array}{r} 6 \\ -\ 6 \\ \hline 0 \end{array}$$
or
$$\begin{array}{r} 6 \\ -\ 0 \\ \hline 6 \end{array}$$

Cut out the numbers 1 to 6 from the bottom of the page.

Place them in the blanks so that the numbers along each line add up to 10.

Record your finding.

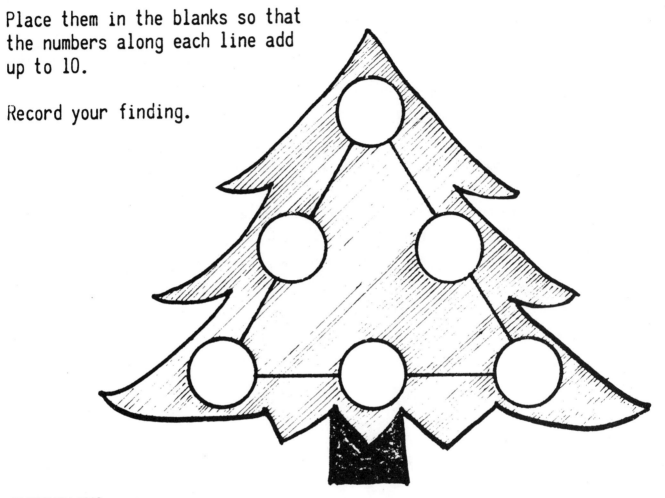

EXTENSIONS

Make each side add up to   * 9.
*11.
*12.

Record your findings on the back of this page.

<u>Trim</u> <u>The</u> <u>Tree</u>

Mathematics teaching objectives:

- Practice basic addition facts.

Problem-solving skills pupils <u>might</u> use:

- Guess and check.
- Look for a pattern.
- Eliminate possibilities.

Materials:

- One pair of scissors for each pupil

Comments and suggestions:

- Make certain pupils understand the directions, then have them complete the page, working alone or with a partner.
- When most of the pupils have completed at least part of no. 2, discuss results as a class. Pupils should note that the smaller numbers are used in the "corner" position when small sums are required, while the larger numbers are used in the corners to produce larger sums.

Answers:

```
        3
      2   6
    5   4   1
```

Extensions: Sum of 9   Sum of 11   Sume of 12

```
          3                    6                      4
        5   4                1   3                  2   3
      1   6   2            4   5   2              6   1   5
```

BELL RINGER PUZZLE

Cut out the numbers
1 to 7 from the bottom
of the page.

Place them in
the blanks so
that the numbers
in each line add
up to 12.

Record your finding.

EXTENSION

Make each line add up to 11.
Record.

Bell Ringer Puzzle

Mathematics teaching objectives:

. Use basic addition facts.

Problem-solving skills pupils might use:

. Guess and check.

. Look for a pattern.

. Eliminate possibilities.

Materials needed:

. One pair of scissors for each pupil

Comments and suggestions:

. Make certain pupils understand the directions, then have them complete
the page on their own or by working with a partner.

. When most pupils have completed the page, discuss solutions. Have
various pupils explain _how_ they solved the puzzles.

Answers:

1.
```
        5 —— 7
       /       \
      1         3
     /           \
    6 —— 4 —— 2
```

2.
```
        4 —— 7
       /       \
      5         1
     /           \
    2 —— 6 —— 3
```

SPELLING FOR DOLLARS

1. Suppose letters were money.

A = $1	F = $6	K = $11	P = $16	U = $21
B = $2	G = $7	L = $12	Q = $17	V = $22
C = $3	H = $8	M = $13	R = $18	W = $23
D = $4	I = $9	N = $14	S = $19	X = $24
E = $5	J = $10	O = $15	T = $20	Y = $25
				Z = $26

   Use the chart. Find out how much "monster" is worth. _____

2. Pick a letter of the alphabet. Write that letter here: _____
   Find words <u>beginning</u> <u>with</u> <u>the</u> <u>letter</u> <u>you</u> <u>picked</u>. Finish the chart below.

Requirement	Word
a. Worth less than $25	
b. Worth between $24 and $36	
c. Worth between $35 and $51	
d. Worth between $50 and $75	
e. Worth between $74 and $101	
f. Worth more than $100	

3. Find as many words as you can worth between $100 and $140.

<u>Spelling</u> <u>For</u> <u>Dollars</u>

Mathematics teaching objectives:

- Practice mental addition and writing column addition of 1- and 2-digit numbers.

Problem-solving skills pupils <u>might</u> use:

- Guess and check.
- Make reasonable estimates.
- Use an organized list.
- Eliminate possibilities.

Materials needed:

- None

Comments and suggestions:

- Discuss the first problem with the class. Pupils usually are interested in finding out who has the most and least expensive names in the class.
- Pupils should be able to complete the remainder of the page on their own or by working with a partner.
- Allow some time to discuss and compare answers.

Answers:

Answers will vary.

MAKE 25¢

Finish the list below. Show ways to make 25¢.
● Hint: Some are <u>not</u> possible.

	Dime	Nickel	Penny
3 coins			
4 coins			
5 coins			
6 coins			
7 coins			
8 coins			
9 coins			
10 coins			
11 coins			
● 12 coins			
13 coins			
14 coins			
15 coins			
16 coins			
17 coins			
18 coins			
19 coins			
20 coins			
21 coins			
22 coins			
23 coins			
24 coins			
● 25 coins			

© PSM 81

Make 25¢

Mathematics teaching objectives:

. Practice mental addition using coin values (dime, nickel, penny).

Problem-solving skillls pupils <u>might</u> use:

. Guess and check.

. Make an organized list.

Materials needed:

. None

Comments and suggestions:

. Make certain pupils understand the directions, then have them complete the page alone or by working with a partner.

. Pupils will enjoy looking for and discussing patterns in the chart of completed data.

Answers:

	10¢	5¢	1¢
3 coins	2	1	
4 coins	1	3	
5 coins		5	
6 coins	Not possible		
7 coins	2		5
8 coins	1	2	5
9 coins	Not possible		
10 coins	Not possible		
11 coins	Not possible		
12 coins	1	1	10
13 coins		3	10
14 coins	Not possible		
15 coins	Not possible		
16 coins	1		15
17 coins		2	15
18 coins	Not possible		
19 coins	Not possible		
20 coins	Not possible		
21 coins		1	20
22 coins	Not possible		
23 coins	Not possible		
24 coins	Not possible		
25 coins			25

CHANGE FOR A DOLLAR

1. Make change for a dollar.
   Use 3 coins.
   Record your findings. _____ _____ _____

2. Make change for a dollar.
   Use 5 coins.
   Make one coin a half-dollar.
   Record. _____ _____ _____ _____ _____

3. Make change for a dollar.
   Use 6 coins.
   Find two different ways.
   Record each way.

   _____ _____ _____ _____ _____ _____

   or

   _____ _____ _____ _____ _____ _____

4. Make change for a dollar.
   Use at least one penny, nickel, dime, quarter, and half-dollar.
   Find and record two different ways.

5. Make change for a dollar.
   Use at least one dime, quarter, and half-dollar. (You may
      also use other coins.)
   How many different ways are possible?
   Find out.
   Record each way.

Change For A Dollar

Mathematics teaching objectives:

. Practice with mental addition.

. Practice using coin values (half-dollar, quarter, dime, nickel, penny) and making change.

Problem-solving skills pupils might use:

. Guess and check.

. Make a systematic list.

. Eliminate possibilities.

. Work backwards.

Materials needed:

. None

Comments and suggestions:

. Discuss nos. 1 and 2 as a class, perhaps using real coins to "show" answers. Have pupils complete the remainder of the page on their own or by working with a partner.

. Real coins or toy money would be helpful for pupils who are having difficulty with the problems.

. Nos. 4 and 5 can be solved with the use of a systematic list. If some pupils are trying to solve the problems without a list or have not set up a list systematically, you may want to give them individual help.

. When most pupils have finished, discuss and compare results. Have pupils explain how they solved the various problems.

. Emphasize again, if necessary, the usefulness of an organized list in solving problems such as nos. 4 and 5.

Answers:

1. half-dollar, quarter, quarter

2. half-dollar, quarter, dime, dime, nickel

3. half-dollar, dime, dime, dime, dime, dime   or
   quarter, quarter, quarter, dime, dime, nickel   or
   half-dollar, quarter, dime, nickel, nickel, nickel

4. 1 half-dollar, 1 quarter, 1 dime, 2 nickels, 5 pennies   and
   1 half-dollar, 1 quarter, 1 dime, 1 nickel, 10 pennies

5.

half-dollar	quarter	dime	nickel	penny
1	1	2	1	0
1	1	2	0	5
1	1	1	3	0
1	1	1	2	5
1	1	1	1	10
1	1	1	0	15

Extension: Make change for a dollar. Use only dimes and/or nickels. How many different ways are possible?

-248-

1. Here are some 3-floor wigwams.   Finish these 3-floor wigwams.

a.
```
   11
  7  4
 4  3  1
```

b.
```
    12
   6  6
  5  1  5
```

c.
```
   4  5
  3  1  4
```

d.
```
  6  2  4
```

2. Finish these 4-floor wigwams.

a.
```
   9  8
  4  5  3  4
```

b.
```
        5
  5  3  3  2
```

c.
```
          4
  6  2     3
```

d.
```
        10
  3  5  7
```

e.
```
   25
      11
   7
  3        1
```

f.
```
    21
          8
  3        6
```

EXTENSION

Use the back of this page. Make up your own 4-floor wigwam puzzles for your classmates to solve.

Make - some with all the numbers on the bottom floor given.
      - some where the given numbers are scattered.

Wigwam Puzzles - B

Mathematics teaching objectives:

- Practice addition and subtraction skills.
- Use mental arithmetic.

Problem-solving skills pupils might use:

- Guess and check.
- Work backwards.
- Eliminate possibilities.

Materials needed:

- None

Commments and suggestions:

- Work the problems in part 1 together. Be certain pupils understand how the "upper floor" numbers are determined. Have pupils complete the remaining problems on their own.

- Pupils who have difficulty with part e in no. 2 may need encouragement to work the problem backwards.

- Problem f in that section may stump some pupils. Encourage such pupils to guess, check, and refine.

Answers:

1.   c.   d.

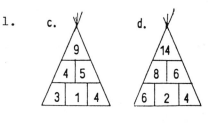

2.   a.   b.   c.

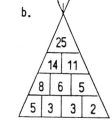   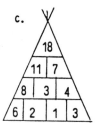

     d.   e.   f.

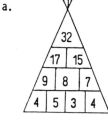   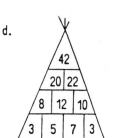   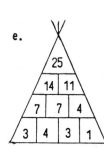   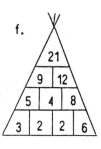

CIRCLES AROUND THE SQUARE

The numbers in the circles around a square are added to get the number in the square.

$6 + 8 + 7 = 21$
$6 + 8 + 9 = 23$
$7 + 8 + 10 = 25$
$8 + 9 + 10 = 27$

1. Cut out the numbers 1 to 5 from the bottom of the page.

   Place them in the circles to get each sum in the squares.

   Record your results.

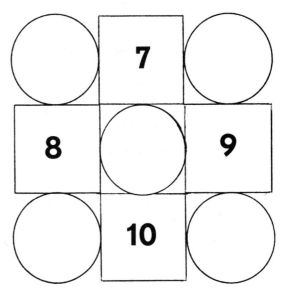

2. Now use the digits 1 to 8 in the circle to get each sum in the squares. Record your results.

   a.   b.

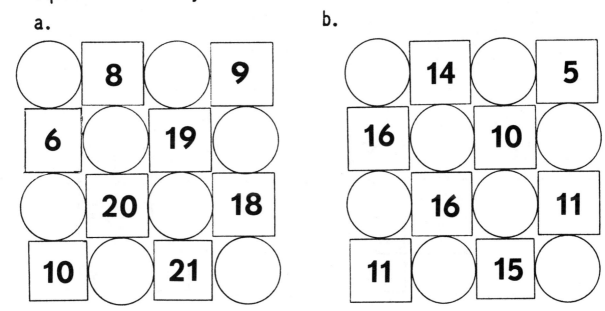

Circles Around The Squares

Mathematics teaching objective:

. Practice adding and subtracting.

Problem-solving skills pupils might use:

. Guess and check.

. Work backwards.

. Eliminate possibilities.

Materials needed:

. None

Comments and suggestions:

. Work problem 7 as a class. Have pupils complete the page on their own or by working with a partner.

. Discuss and compare solutions to completed problems. Have various pupils explain how they solved the problems.

Extension:

Pupils who finish ahead of others could be asked to make up their own "Circles Around Squares" puzzles.

Answers:

1.

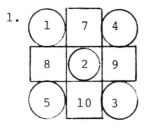

2-a.

2-b.

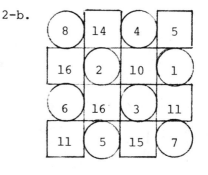

WHEELS

1. Cut out the numbers 1 to 7 below.
   Place them in the spaces of the puzzle.
   Make each line add up to 12.

2. Use the numbers 1 to 9.
   Make each line add up to 15.

EXTENSION

Use the back of this page. Make up your own wheel puzzle.

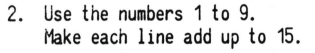

<u>Wheels</u>

Mathematics teaching objectives:

. Practice mental addition.

Problem-solving skills pupils <u>might</u> use:

. Guess and check.

. Look for a pattern.

Materials needed:

. One pair of scissors for each pupil or pair of pupils

Comments and suggestions:

. Use as a challenge problem or problem of the week.

. If class time is provided to work on the activity, encourage pupils to work in pairs.

Answers:

1.

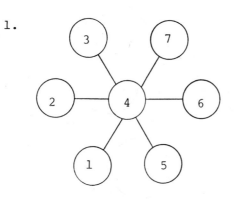

2.

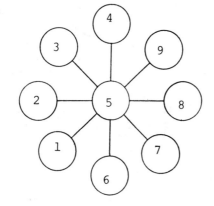

Extension: Answers will vary.

PUZZLE PROBLEMS

1. Cut out the numbers
    1 to 5 below.

    Place them in the
    spaces of the puzzle.

    Make each line add
    up to 9.

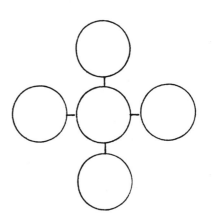

2.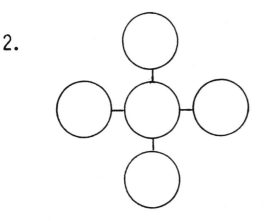

Use the numbers 2 to 6.

Place them in the spaces of
the puzzle.

Make each line add up to 12.

EXTENSION

Use the numbers
5, 6, 7, 8, 9.

Place them in the spaces
so that all 3 numbers in
a line equal the same sum.

| 1 | 2 | 3 | 4 | 5 | 6 | 7 | 8 | 9 |

Puzzle Problems

Mathematics teaching objectives:

. Practice mental addition.

Problem-solving skills pupils <u>might</u> use:

. Guess and check.

. Look for a pattern.

Materials needed:

. One pair of scissors for each pupil or pair of pupils

Comments and suggestions:

. Use as a challenge problem or problem of the week.

. If time is provided in class to work on the activity, encourage pupils to work in pairs.

Answers:

1.   2.

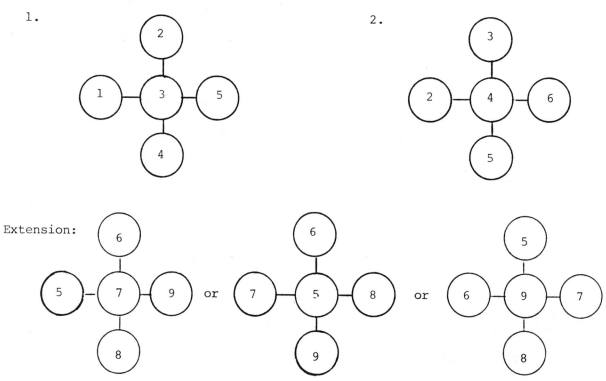

Extension: Have pupils make up their own puzzle problems similar to these.

PUZZLERS

1. Cut out the numbers 1 to 5 from the bottom of the page.

   Place them in the spaces so that the numbers along each line add up to 9.

   Record your finding.

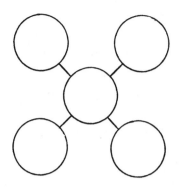

2.

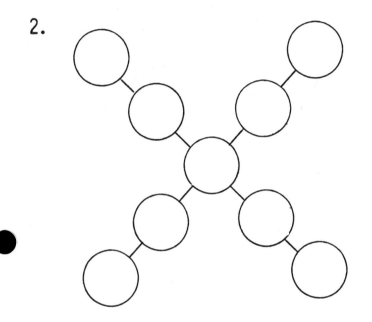

Use the numbers 1 to 9.

Make the numbers along each line of this puzzle add up to 27.

Record your finding.

EXTENSIONS:

Using the puzzle in problem 2,

. place the numbers 3 to 11 in the spaces to make equal sums on each line.

. use the numbers 5 to 13. Make the sums on each line equal.

Puzzlers

Mathematics teaching objectives:

. Practice mental addition.

Problem-solving skills pupils might use:

. Guess and check.

. Look for a pattern.

Materials needed:

. One pair of scissors for each pupil or pair of pupils.

Comments and suggestions:

. Use as a challenge problem or problem of the week.

. If time is provided in class to work on the activity, encourage pupils to work in pairs.

Answers:

1.

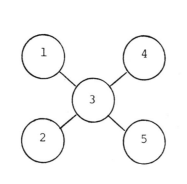

2.

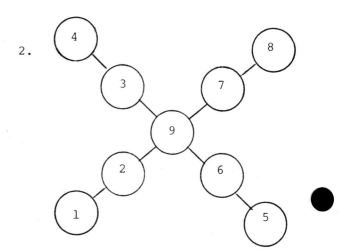

Extensions: Answers can vary. Two possibilities are shown.

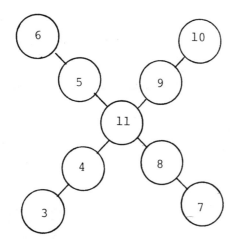

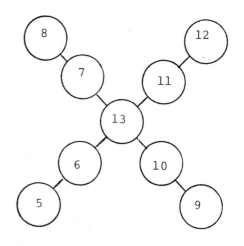

DART PROBLEMS

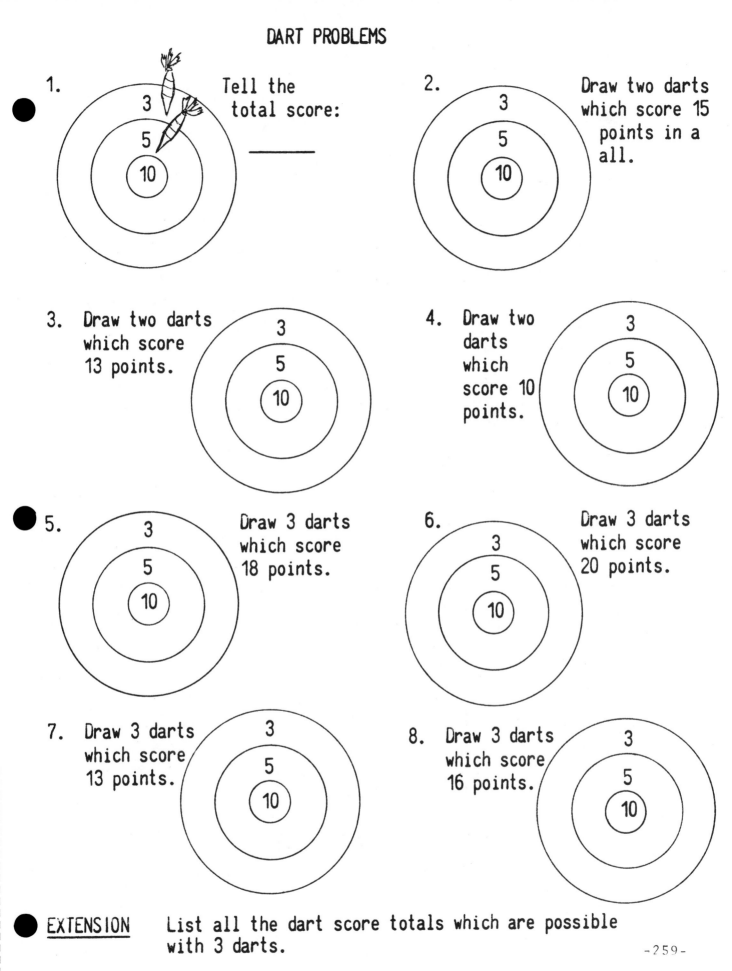

1. Tell the total score:

____

2. Draw two darts which score 15 points in a all.

3. Draw two darts which score 13 points.

4. Draw two darts which score 10 points.

5. Draw 3 darts which score 18 points.

6. Draw 3 darts which score 20 points.

7. Draw 3 darts which score 13 points.

8. Draw 3 darts which score 16 points.

EXTENSION   List all the dart score totals which are possible with 3 darts.

-259-

Dart Problems

Mathematics teaching objectives:

. Practice mental addition.

Problem-solving skills pupils might use:

. Guess and check.

. Make an organized list.

Materials needed:

. None

Comments and suggestions:

. Discuss directions and do first two examples as a class.

. Have pupils complete the remainder of the activity on their own.

. Discuss and compare answers. If possible, work through the extension activity together.

Answers:

1. 8 points

2. 5 and 10

3. 10 and 3

4. two 5's

5. 10, 5, and 3

6. 10 and two 5's

7. two 5's and a 3

8. one 10 and two 3's

Extension:

10	5	3	Total
✓ ✓ ✓			30
✓ ✓	✓		25
✓ ✓		✓	23
✓	✓ ✓		20
✓	✓	✓	18
✓		✓ ✓	16
	✓ ✓ ✓		15
	✓ ✓	✓	13
	✓	✓ ✓	11
		✓ ✓ ✓	9

10 different totals

TARGET TOTALS

1. Find and circle two numbers whose sum is the number shown at the top of each puzzle.

   Check your work with a calculator.

   a.

100		
12	18	21
24	35	46
76	80	90

   b.

136		
12	18	21
24	35	46
76	80	90

   c.

122		
12	18	21
24	35	46
76	80	90

2. Find and circle <u>three</u> numbers whose sum is given.

   a.

265		
10	22	43
55	72	90
120	150	200

   b.

312		
10	22	43
55	72	90
120	150	200

   c.

360		
10	22	43
55	72	90
120	150	200

   d.

400		
10	25	50
70	75	80
125	155	210
250	280	360

   e.

560		
10	25	50
70	75	80
125	155	210
250	280	360

   f.

610		
10	25	50
70	75	80
125	155	210
250	280	360

3. Find two different sets of <u>three</u> numbers whose sum is 1000.

1000			
540	320	290	600
490	80	600	310
370	160	250	750
100	700	400	800

<u>Target</u> <u>Totals</u>

Mathematics teaching objectives:

. Mentally add 2- and 3-digit numbers.

. Use place value concepts to make reasonable estimates.

Problem-solving skills pupils <u>might</u> use:

. Guess and check.

. Make reasonable estimates.

Materials needed:

. One calculator for each pair of pupils (optional)

Comments and suggestions:

. Work the problems in part 1 as a whole-class activity. Review rounding
and use of the "make a reasonable estimate" skill.

. Once pupils understand the task, have them complete the page, working in
pairs or individually.

. Compare solutions and strategies as a class.

Answers:

1. a. 24 and 76

    b. 46 and 90

    c. 76 and 46

2. a. 22, 43, 200

    b. 22, 90, 200

    c. 90, 120, 150

    d. 25, 125, 250

    e. 75, 125, 360

    f. 80, 250, 280

3. 320, 80, and 600   and   290, 310, and 400

REGULAR TRIANGULAR PATTERNS-1

1. Use the numbers in the top row.
   Follow the arrows. Add each pair
   Find the final sum for the bottom
   box.

   a.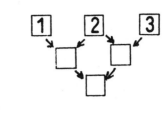

   b.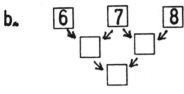

   c.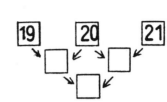

2. Predict the final sum before you add. Look for patterns in a-c above.

   a. Prediction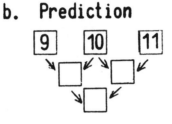

   b. Prediction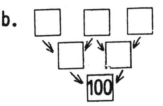

   c. Prediction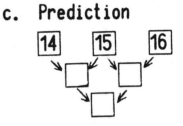

3. The final sum is given. Find the other numbers.

   a.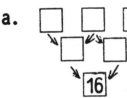

   b.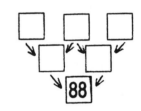

   c.

4. Find these final sums.

   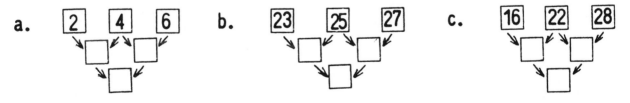

5. Write a statement to tell how to find the final sum of a regular 3-row triangular pattern.

<u>Regular</u> <u>Triangular</u> <u>Patters</u> - 1

Mathematics teaching objectives:

. Practice adding one- and two-digit numbers mentally.

Problem-solving skills <u>pupils</u> might use:

. Guess and check.

. Look for a pattern.

. Work backwards.

Materials needed:

. None

Comments and suggestions:

. Work problem 1 together. Make sure pupils understand the directions, then have them complete the page on their own or by working with a partner. Encourage pupils to make predictions before solving the problems in parts 2, 3, and 4.

. Discuss results and solution strategies as a class.

Answers:

1. a.   1   2   3   b.   6   7   8:   c.   19 20 21
          3   5   13 15   39 41
            8   28   80

2. a.   7   8   9   b.   9 10 11   c.   14 15 16
          15 17   19 21   29 31
            32   40   60

3. Pupils will probably give the answers below. (Other answers are possible.)

    a.   3   4   5   b.   24 25 26   c.   21 22 23
          7   9   49 51   43 45
           16   100   88

4. a. 2   4   6   b.   23 25 27   c.   16 22 28
         6 10   48 52   38 50
          16   100   88

5. To find the final sum of a regular 3-row triangular puzzle, multiply the middle number in the top row by 4.

-264-

REGULAR TRIANGULAR PATTERNS-2

1. Use the numbers in the top row. Follow the arrows. Add each pair. Find the final sum for the bottom box.

a.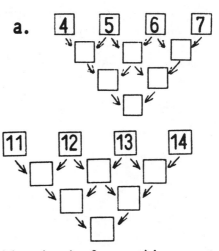

b.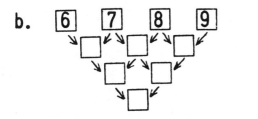

c.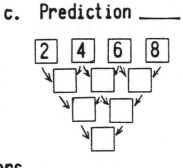

2. Predict the final sum before you add. Look for patterns in a-c above.

a. Prediction _____ b. Prediction _____ c. Prediction _____

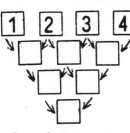

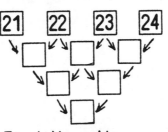

3. The final sum is given. Find the other numbers.

a. 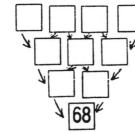 28

b. 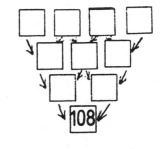 68

c. 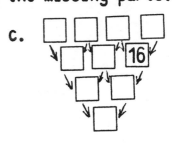 108

4. These are regular triangular patterns. Find the missing parts.

a. 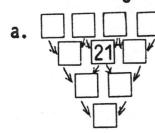 21

b. 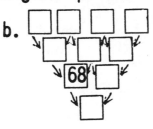 68

c. 16

Regular Triangular Patterns - 2

Mathematics teaching objective:

. Practice mental addition of one- and two-digit numbers.

Problem-solving skills pupils might use:

. Guess and check.

. Look for a pattern.

. Work backwards.

Materials needed:

. None

Comments and suggestions:

. Work the three problems in part 1 as a class. Be certain pupils understand the directions, then have them complete the page on their own or by working with a partner. Encourage pupils to make predictions before completing each of the puzzles.

. Discuss and compare completed puzzles. Ask pupils to explain the strategies used to complete each of the puzzles.

Answers:

1. a. 4   5   6   7   b. 6   7   8   9   c. 11   12   13   14
      9 11 13   13 15 17   23   25   27
        20 24   28 32   48   52
          44   60   100

2. a. 1   2   3   4   b. 21   22   23   24   c. 2   4   6   8
      3   5   7   43   45   47   6 10 14
        8 12   88 92   16 24
         20   180   40

3. Pupils probably will give the answers below.
      a. 2   3   4   5   b. 7   8   9   10   c. 12   13   14   15
          5   7   9   15 17 19   25   27   29
           12 15   32 36   52   56
             28   68   108

4. (Other answers are possible.)
      a. 9   10   11   12   b. 16   17   18   19   c. 3   5   7   9
         19   21   23   33   35   37   8 12 16
           40 44   68 72   20 28
             84   140   48

-266-

IRREGULAR TRIANGULAR PATTERNS

1. Use the numbers in the top row.
   Follow the arrows. Add each pair.
   Find the final sum for the bottom
   box.

   a.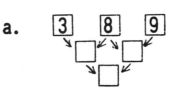

   b.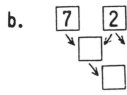

   c.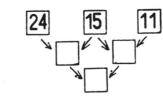

2. Find the missing parts.

   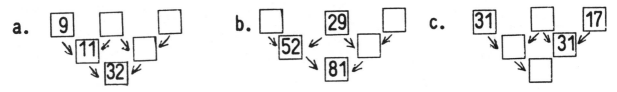

   a.   b.   c.

3. Create three different 3-row patterns with a final sum of 42.

   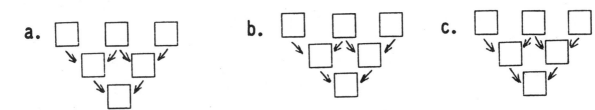

   a.   b.   c.

4. Create three different 4-row patterns with a final sum of 42.

   a. 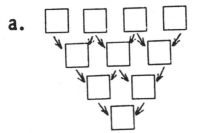   b.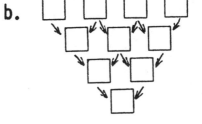

   c.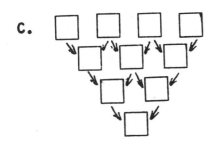

Irregular Triangular Patterns

Mathematics teaching objectives:

. Practice mental addition and subtraction of one- and two-digit numbers.

Problem-solving skills pupils <u>might</u> use:

. Guess and check.

. Look for a pattern.

. Work backwards.

Materials needed:

. None

Comments and suggestions:

. Work the examples in problem 1 as a class. Have pupils complete the remainder of the page on their own or by working with a partner.

. When most pupils have completed the page, discuss answers. Have various pupils explain how they solved the puzzles and how they created new 3- and 4-row puzzles.

. If pupils have completed the "Regular Triangular Patterns" worksheets, have them compare the two kinds of puzzles. Ask:

    - Which are easier to solve?

    - Can final sums on both be predicted?

    - Do you use the same problem-solving skills to solve each?

Answers:

1. a.   3 8 9   b.   7 2 15   c.   24 15 11
          11 17   9 17   39 26
            28   26   65

2. a.   9 2 19   b. 23 29 0   c. 31 14 17
         11 21   52 29   45 31
           32   81   76

3. a-c. Answers will vary.

4. a-c. Answers will vary.

RHYMING RULER

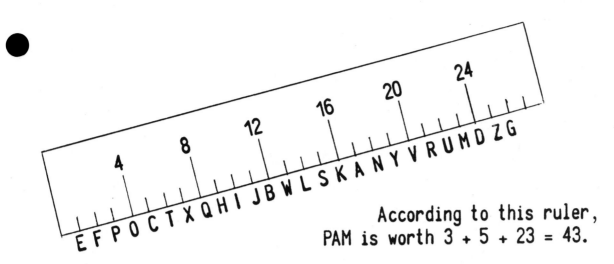

According to this ruler,
PAM is worth 3 + 5 + 23 = 43.

1. According to this ruler, which is worth more? How much more?

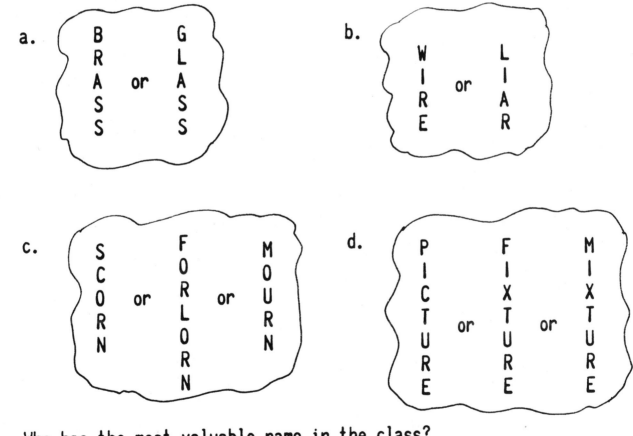

a. B R A S S   or   G L A S S

b. W I R E   or   L I A R

c. S C O R N   or   F O R L O R N   or   M O U R N

d. P I C T U R E   or   F I X T U R E   or   M I X T U R E

2. Who has the most valuable name in the class?

3. What is the most valuable 3-letter word on the ruler?

4. Create your own question to ask.

-269-

<u>Rhyming</u> <u>Ruler</u>

Mathematics teaching objective:

. Practice adding whole numbers.

Problem-solving skills pupils <u>might</u> use:

. Guess and check.

. Look for a pattern.

. Break a problem into parts.

. Create new problems by varying a given one.

Materials needed:

. None

Comments and suggestions:

. Introduce the activity with the overhead projector. Find the "value" of
several pupils' names. Then have pupils complete the page on their own
or by working with a partner.

. The words on this activity are written in vertical form. This helps
pupils to place the values vertically and makes adding easier.

Answers:

1. a. GLASS = 87; BRASS = 80
        GLASS is worth 7 more.

   b. WIRE = 45; LIAR = 62
        LIAR is worth 17 more.

   c. SCORN = 63; FORLORN = 84; MOURN = 88
        MOURN is worth 4 more than FORLORN and 25 more than SCORN.

   d. PICTURE = 68; FIXTURE = 69; MIXTURE = 90
        MIXTURE is worth 21 more than FIXTURE and 22 more than PICTURE.

2. Answers will vary.

3. GAG = 69
   DUG = 72   } Here are some "expense" 3-letter words on this
   GUM or MUG = 71 }   ruler.

4. Answers will vary.

Extension:

Find out which teachers in your building has the name with the greatest
value.

45 2 3 12 48 6 8 14 25 33

3 35 18 4 72 42 30 56 3 44

15 5 10 9 12 5 28 11 17 35

72 38 8 36 6 6 4 27 31 5

48 8 $\times$ 80 4 20 (11 − 7 = 4) 9 36

64 = 4 24 8 3 5 15 45 40 3

7 13 12 32 35 19 8 3 6 18

32 33 28 4 7 (6 = 9) 4 19 21

58 18 40 36 (3 + 7) 21 28 36 4

25 54 37 26 63 13 49 57 20 25

3 72 (17 = 4 + 7 + 6) 52 2 26 50

MAKE AND "LOOP" CORRECT NUMBER SENTENCES.

Number Sentence Search

Mathematics teaching objectives:

- Practice solving addition, subtraction, multiplication, and division problems and chain calculations.
- Recognize addition/subtraction and multiplication/division relationships.

Problem-solving skills pupils might use:

- Guess and check.
- Look for a pattern.
- Search through printed materials for pertinent data.

Materials needed:

- Transparency made from activity page
- Overhead projector
- AV pen or pencil

Comments and suggestions:

- Display transparency of the activity page on the overhead screen or chalkboard.
- Ask pupils to search for and identify true mathematical statements such as those already looped.
- As pupils identify such statements, loop them with the AV pen or pencil.
- Note that for each addition statement a related subtraction fact could have been created instead. Note similar multiplication/division relationships. (Example: $64 = 8 \times 8$ and $64 \div 8 = 8$)

Answers:

Answers will vary.

MULTIPLICATION CUT-UPS – A

Cut out the numbers 0 to 9 from the bottom of the page.
Place them in the spaces below. Use each number one time only.
Make each multiplication problem correct.
Record your findings.

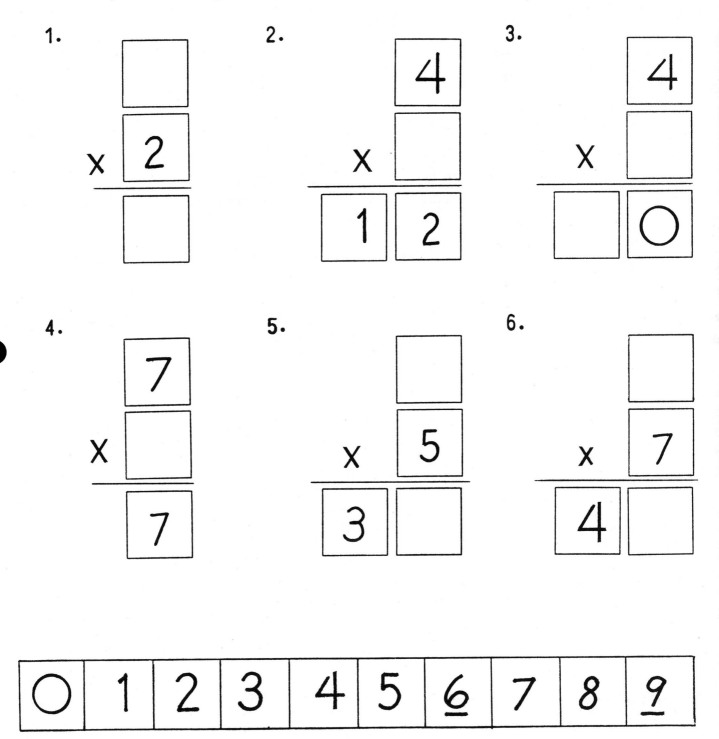

Multiplication Cut-Ups - A

Mathematics teaching objective:

. Practice with basic multiplication facts.

Problem-solving skills pupils might use:

. Guess and check.

. Work backwards.

. Eliminate possibilities.

Materials needed:

. One pair of scissors for each pupil

Comments and suggestions:

. Be certain pupils understand the general directions and then ask them to complete the page on their own.

. Pupils who are having difficulty may be encouraged to find and solve first those problems that have only one possible answer, i.e., nos. 2, 3, and 4.

Answers:

1.
$$\begin{array}{r} 4 \\ \times\ 2 \\ \hline 8 \end{array}$$

2.
$$\begin{array}{r} 4 \\ \times\ 3 \\ \hline 12 \end{array}$$

3.
$$\begin{array}{r} 4 \\ \times\ 5 \\ \hline 20 \end{array}$$

4.
$$\begin{array}{r} 7 \\ \times\ 1 \\ \hline 7 \end{array}$$

5.
$$\begin{array}{r} 6 \\ \times\ 5 \\ \hline 30 \end{array}$$

6.
$$\begin{array}{r} 7 \\ \times\ 7 \\ \hline 49 \end{array}$$

MULTIPLICATION CUT-UPS - B

Cut out the numbers 0 to 9 from the bottom of the page.
Place them in the spaces below. Use each number one time only.
Make each multiplication problem correct.
Record your findings.

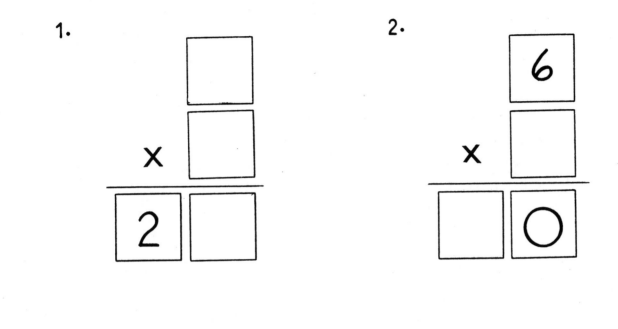

1.

2.

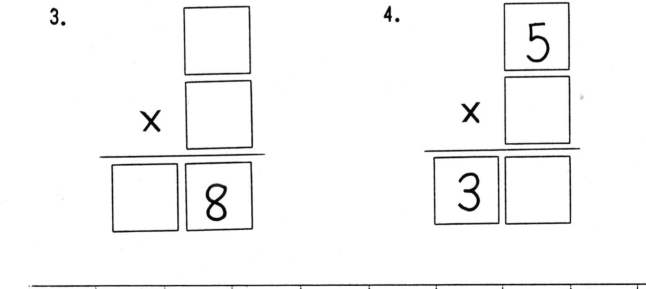

3.

4.

<u>Multiplication Cut-Ups</u> - <u>B</u>

Mathematics teaching objective:

. Practice with basic multiplication facts.

Problem-solving skills pupils <u>might</u> use:

. Guess and check.

. Work backwards.

. Eliminate possibilities.

Materials needed:

. One pair of scissors for each pupil

Comments and suggestions:

. Be certain pupils understand the general directions and then ask them
to complete the page on their own.

. Pupils who are having difficulty may be encouraged to find and solve
first the problem which has only one possible answer, i.e., no. 2.

Answers:

1.
$$\begin{array}{r} 7 \\ \times\ 4 \\ \hline 28 \end{array}$$

2.
$$\begin{array}{r} 6 \\ \times\ 5 \\ \hline 30 \end{array}$$

3.
$$\begin{array}{r} 9 \\ \times\ 2 \\ \hline 18 \end{array}$$

4.
$$\begin{array}{r} 5 \\ \times\ 6 \\ \hline 30 \end{array}$$

MULTIPLICATION CUT-UPS - C

Cut out the numbers 0 to 9 from the bottom of the page.
Place them in the spaces below.
Make each multiplication problem correct.
Record your findings.

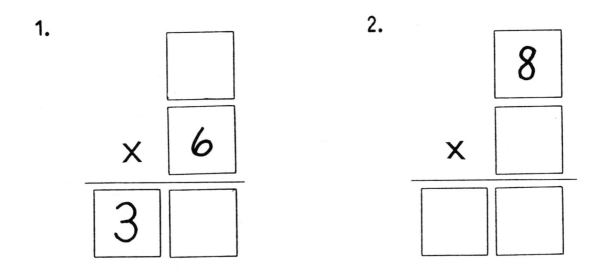

1.

2.

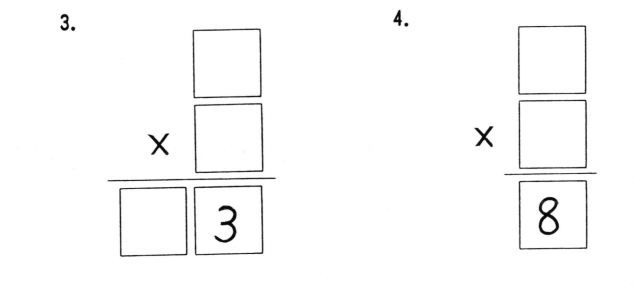

3.

4.

| ◯ | 1 | 2 | 3 | 4 | 5 | 6 | 7 | 8 | 9 |

© PSM 81

<u>Multiplication</u> <u>Cut-Ups</u> - <u>C</u>

Mathematics teaching objectives:

. Practice with basic multiplication facts.

Problem-solving skills pupils <u>might</u> use:

. Guess and check.

. Work backwards.

. Eliminate possibilities.

Materials needed:

. One pair of scissors for each pupil

Comments and suggestions:

. Be certain pupils understand the general directions and then ask them
to complete the page on their own.

Answers:

1.
$$
\begin{array}{r}
5 \\
\times\ 6 \\
\hline
30
\end{array}
$$

2.
$$
\begin{array}{r}
8 \\
\times\ 4 \\
\hline
32
\end{array}
$$

3.
$$
\begin{array}{r}
9 \\
\times\ 7 \\
\hline
63
\end{array}
$$
or
$$
\begin{array}{r}
7 \\
\times\ 9 \\
\hline
63
\end{array}
$$

4.
$$
\begin{array}{r}
1 \\
\times\ 8 \\
\hline
8
\end{array}
$$
or
$$
\begin{array}{r}
8 \\
\times\ 1 \\
\hline
8
\end{array}
$$

MULTIPLICATION TRIANGLE PUZZLES - B

1. Here are some 3-story triangle puzzles.   Finish these:

a. 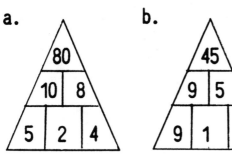 b. c. 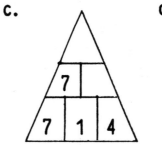 d.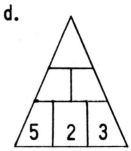

2. Finish these triangle puzzles.

a. 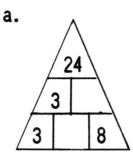 b. 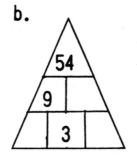 c.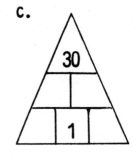

3. Finish these:

a. 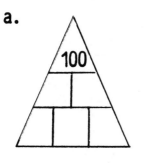 b. 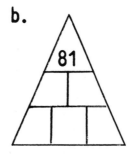 c.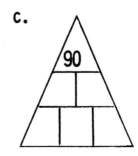

4. Finish these 2 different ways.

a. 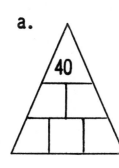 b. 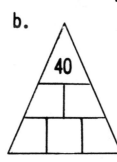 c. 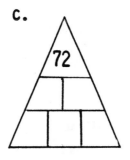 d.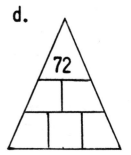

Multiplication Triangle Puzzles - B

Mathematics teaching objectives:

. Practice basic multiplication facts.

. Use mental arithmetic.

Problem-solving skills pupils <u>might</u> use:

. Guess and check.

. Work backwards.

. Eliminate possibilities.

. Search for another answer.

Materials needed:

. None

Comments and suggestions:

. Work several problems together as a class, then have pupils complete the page by working on their own or with a partner.

. Many of the problems on this page have more than one right answer. Be sure to discuss this fact when summarizing the lesson with pupils.

Answers:

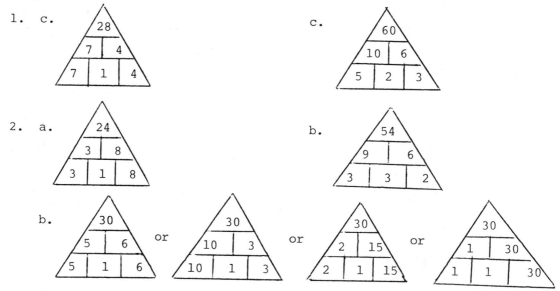

1. c.

   28
   7 | 4
   7 | 1 | 4

   c.

   60
   10 | 6
   5 | 2 | 3

2. a.

   24
   3 | 8
   3 | 1 | 8

   b.

   54
   9 | 6
   3 | 3 | 2

   b.

   30
   5 | 6
   5 | 1 | 6

   or

   30
   10 | 3
   10 | 1 | 3

   or

   30
   2 | 15
   2 | 1 | 15

   or

   30
   1 | 30
   1 | 1 | 30

3. a-c. Many correct answers are possible.

4. a and b. Many correct answers are possible.

Extension:

   Have pupils make up 3-story triangle puzzles -

   . some with all the numbers on the bottom story given.

   . some where the given numbers are scattered.

   . some with more than one right answer.

1. In each puzzle below

    . Use any of these numbers: 0, 1, 2, 3, 4, 5, 6, 7, 8, 9.

    . Use a number only one time.

    . Fill in the circles. Make both the sum of the numbers
      going across and the sum of the numbers going down
      multiples of 3 (3, 6, 9, 12, etc.).

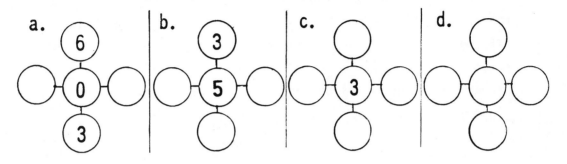

2. Make both sums multiples of 4.

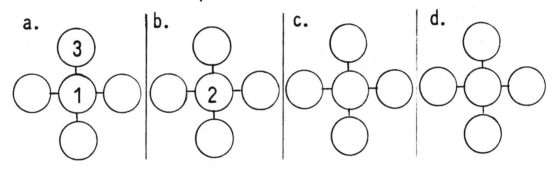

3. Make both sums multiples of 5.

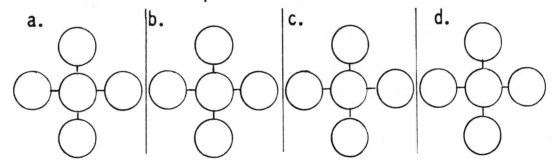

EXTENSION

Make up your own Cross Sum puzzles with multiples.

Cross Sums - B

Mathematics teaching objectives:

. Practice adding single-digit numbers.

. Practice with multiples of 3, 4, and 5.

Problem-solving skills pupils might use:

. Guess and check.

. Eliminate possibilities.

Comments and suggestions:

. Work 1-a as a class. Try to find all possible solutions. Remind pupils that other problems on this page may have more than one right answer. (If you wish, challenge pupils to find all possible solutions for each problem.)

. Discuss solutions and "correct" paper together.

Answers:

1. a.

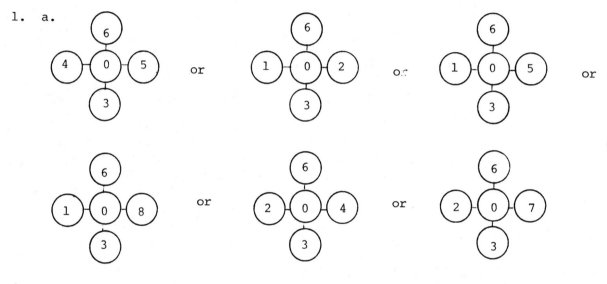

b-d. Answers will vary.

2. a-d. Answers will vary.

3. a-d. Answers will vary.

DECIMAL CLUES

Make up problems to fit the clues below.

Clues

Problem Workspace

1. Two decimals whose sum is 35.6:
   _____ and _____

2. Three decimals whose sum is 23.5:
   _____, _____, and _____

3. Two decimals whose difference is
   5.2: _____ and _____

4. Two decimals whose difference is
   7.31: _____ and _____

5. Three decimals whose sum is 32.01:
   _____, _____, and _____

6. Two decimals whose sum is between
   1 and 2: _____ and _____

7. Three decimals whose sum is between
   11.2 and 11.5: _____,
   _____ and _____

8. Two decimals with a difference
   between 3 and 4: _____ and
   _____

Decimal Clues

Mathematics teaching objectives:

- Practice using estimation skills in decimal addition and subtraction situations.
- practice mental and written decimal addition and subtraction computations.
- Practice solving problems with more than one right answer.
- Use the "between" concept.

Problem-solving skills pupils <u>might</u> use:

- Guess and check.
- Use previously-acquired knowledge.
- Make reasonable estimates.

Materials needed:

- None (Calculators optional for checking work.)

Comments and suggestions:

- Work the first few examples as a class. Be certain pupils are familiar with the words "sum" and "difference" and can use them appropriately. Then have pupils complete the activity on their own or by working with a partner.
- Since correct answers will vary considerably, one method of checking answers is to pair up and check each other's answers, perhaps with calculators.

Answers:

1-8. Answers will vary. Accept any answers that meet the requirements of the activity.

FACTOR CLUES

Make up problems to fit the clues below. Use factors with two digits.
Use the workspace, if needed.

1. Two factors whose product has three
    digits: _____ and _____

2. Two factors whose product has four
    digits: _____ and _____

3. Two factors whose product has five
    digits: _____ and _____

4. Two factors whose product is
    between 550 and 650:

    _____ and _____

5. Two factors whose product is
    between 1000 and 1200:

    _____ and _____

6. Two factors whose product is
    between 1320 and 1420:

    _____ and _____

7. Two factors whose product is
    between 3510 and 3560:

    _____ and _____

Factor Clues

Mathematics teaching objectives:

- Practice estimation.
- Practice using the vocabulary.
- Get mental and written practice with multiplication algorithms.
- Solve problems with more than one right answer.

Problem-solving skills pupils _might_ use:

- Make a reasonable estimate.
- Guess and check.
- Eliminate possibilities.

Materials needed:

- Calculators (optional, for checking work)

Comments and suggestions:

- To introduce the activity, find _multiple solutions_ to the problems below. Encourage pupils to make reasonable estimates as guesses, and then checking.

  - Name two factors whose product is larger than 200 but smaller than 500 (using 2-digit numbers only).
  - Name two factors whose product is about 600 (2-digit numbers).

- If pupils are unsure of the meaning of the terms "factor" and "product," review their meanings.

- When pupils have completed the problems, have them pair up and check each other's answers (using a calculator, if you wish).

Extension:

Pupils who finish ahead of others can make up additional factor clue problems.

Answers:

Answers will vary.

SQUARE DEAL

These are squares: These are <u>not</u> squares:

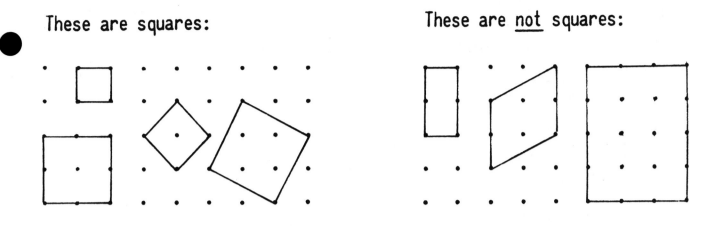

Use a geoboard and 4 rubber bands.

Make as many other different-sized squares as you can. Record each below.

Square Deal

Mathematics teaching objectives:

. Recognize squares and properties of squares.

. Provide informal experience with the concept of similarity.

Problem-solving skills pupils <u>might</u> use:

. Make a model.

. Sort and classify according to properties.

Materials needed:

. One geoboard for each pair of pupils or one for each pupil.

. Four rubber bands (of various colors and sizes, if possible) for each pair of pupils.

Comments and suggestions:

. Pupils can work in pairs on this activity.

. If geoboards are not available, patterns of geoboards reproduced on paper can be substituted.

. Some pupils may need to use a small index card to determine if the polygons they have constructed have <u>square</u> <u>corners</u>.

. As pupils complete the activity, provide encouragement for careful and accurate recording of results.

Answers:

Eight squares are possible. The first four are easily discovered.

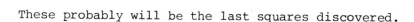

These may be
  more difficult.

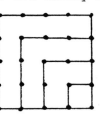

These probably will be the last squares discovered.

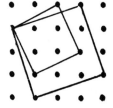

Note: A transparent geoboard for use on an overhead projector is very useful for introducing geoboard activities and for discussing and comparing results.

LINE SEGMENTS

Get a geoboard, some rubber bands, and a metric ruler.

1. Make this line segment on the geoboard.

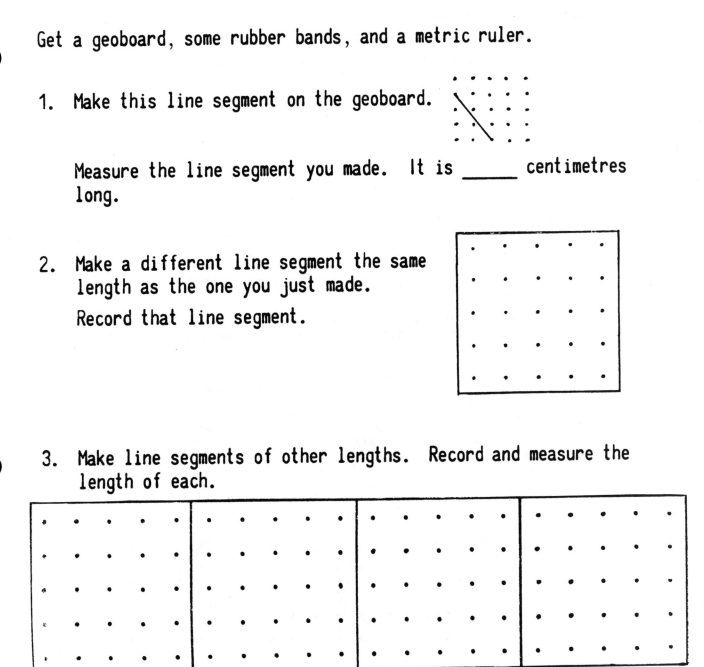

   Measure the line segment you made. It is _____ centimetres long.

2. Make a different line segment the same length as the one you just made.
   Record that line segment.

3. Make line segments of other lengths. Record and measure the length of each.

_____ cm   _____ cm   _____ cm   _____ cm

(Continue on the next page.)

Line Segments

Mathematics teaching objectives:

- Reocgnize and use line segments.
- Use a metric ruler to measure length to the nearest centimeter.

Problem-solving skills pupils might use:

- Make a model.

Materials needed:

- One geoboard and five rubber bands (of various colors and sizes if possible) for each pair of pupils or for each individual pupil.

Comments and suggestions:

- You may want to complete parts 1 and 2 as a class activity. Be certain pupils are measuring correctly and accurately.
- The remainder of the page can be completed individually, or by working in pairs.
- If small geoboards (less than 10") are used, several of the line segments may have the same measure when measured to the nearest centimeter.

Answers:

1 and 2. Answers will vary, depending on the size of geoboard used.

3. Answers will vary, depending on the size of geoboard used. Fourteen different lengths are possible. They are shown on five different record sheets although all can be made using one corner nail on a geoboard. On a geoboard measuring 20 cm between adjacent corner nails, the fourteen lengths were 5, 10, 15, 20, 7, 11, 16, 21, 14, 18, 23, 22, 25, and 29 cm respectively.

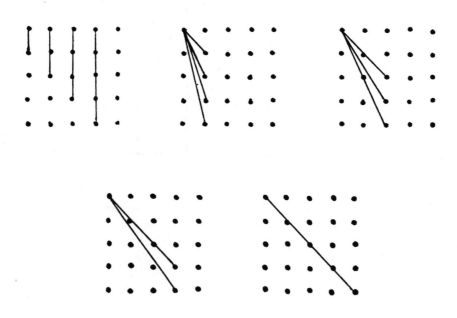

Line Segments (cont.)

_____ cm　　　_____ cm　　　_____ cm　　　_____ cm

_____ cm　　　_____ cm　　　_____ cm　　　_____ cm

_____ cm　　　_____ cm　　　_____ cm　　　_____ cm

BE A BOX BUILDER

1. Jim wanted to draw a shape
   that would fold up to make
   a box <u>without</u> a lid. He drew this shape. ⟶

   Do you think it will make a box with no lid?

   How could you find out for sure?

2. Decide if each of the shapes below will make a box with no lid.
   Record your guesses (Yes or No).

   a. ___   b. ___   c. ___   d. ___   e. ___   f. ___

   Now find out which will actually make boxes without lids.

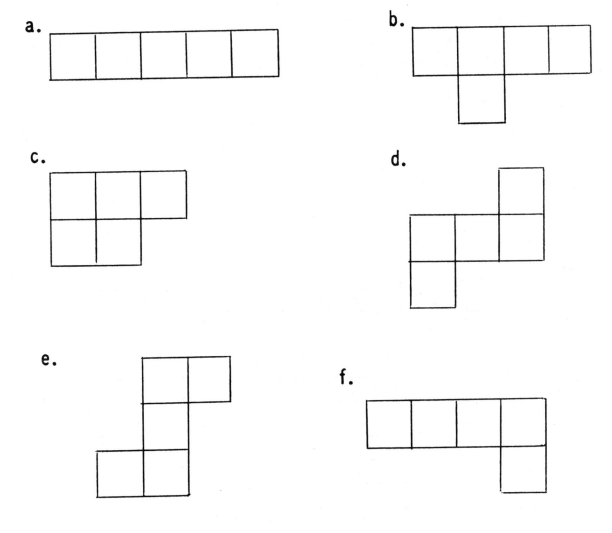

<u>Be</u> <u>A</u> <u>Box</u> <u>Builder</u>

Mathematics teaching objectives:

.   Construct cubes from various nets.

.   Recognize some properties of a cube.

Problem-solving skills pupils <u>might</u> use:

.   Make a model.

.   Guess and check.

Materials needed:

.   Scissors for each pupil or pair of pupils.

Comments and suggestions:

.   Discuss part 1. Pupils will probably suggest that the best way to
    determine if the shape will fold up to make a box without a lid is to
    cut it out and fold it up. Demonstrate this to the class.

.   Have pupils <u>predict</u> answers to part 2; show you their predictions; then
    cut out the shapes and find out which actually do make boxes.

.   Ask pupils to try to complete parts 3 and 4 <u>without</u> cutting out the
    shapes. But have extra copies available so they can eventually cut out
    and "test" their predictions.

Answers:

1.   Yes

2.   a. No   b. yes   c. no   d. yes   e. yes   f. yes

3.   Yes

4.   a. yes   b. no   c. yes   d. yes   e. no   f. yes

For your information, there are eleven shapes that will fold up to make a cube.

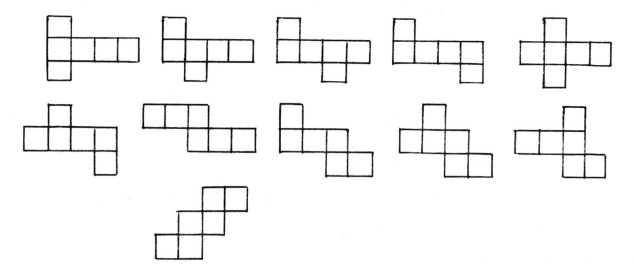

-294-

Be A Box Builder (cont.)

3. This time Jim wants shapes that will
   fold up to make a box <u>with</u> a lid.
   Will the shape to the right work?

   How could you find out for sure?

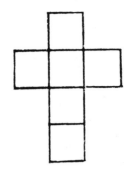

4. Decide if each of the shapes below will make a box with a lid.
   Record your guesses (Yes or No).

   a._____   b. _____   c. _____   d. _____   e. _____   f. _____

   Now find out which will make boxes with lids.

   a.

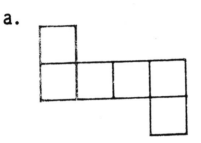

   b.

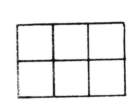

   c.

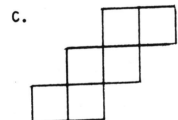

   d.

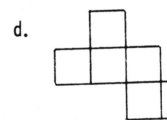

   e.

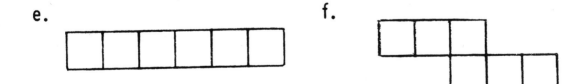

   f.

© PSM 82

POLYHEDRONS

You will need scissors, tape, and 5 shapes sheets.

1. Cut out the shapes on each sheet.
   Tell how many of each shape you have:

   _____ squares   _____ tall triangles

   _____ small triangles   _____ rectangles

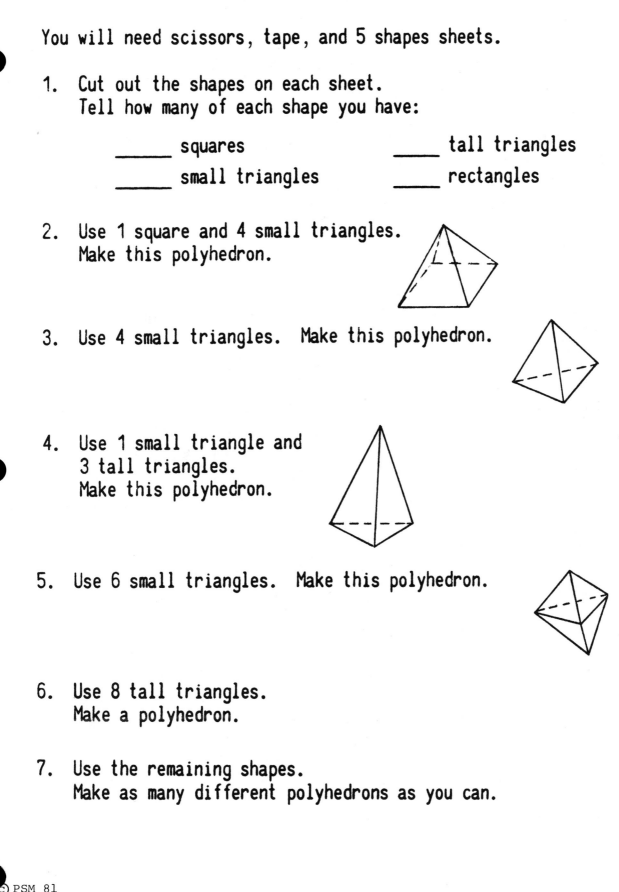

2. Use 1 square and 4 small triangles.
   Make this polyhedron.

3. Use 4 small triangles. Make this polyhedron.

4. Use 1 small triangle and
   3 tall triangles.
   Make this polyhedron.

5. Use 6 small triangles. Make this polyhedron.

6. Use 8 tall triangles.
   Make a polyhedron.

7. Use the remaining shapes.
   Make as many different polyhedrons as you can.

Polyhedrons

Mathematics teaching objectives:

. Develop three-dimensional concepts.

. Construct polyhedrons by using two-dimensional shapes.

Problem-solving skills pupils might use:

. Make a model.

. Visualize an object from its drawing.

Materials needed:

. Each pupil will need scissors, tape (transparent or masking), and
   four "shapes sheets" (see pattern sheet following this lesson).

Comments and suggestions:

. Use the "shapes sheet" pattern. Reproduce about 150 copies
   (or 5 per pupil) on construction paper or oaktag.

. Have pupils work with a partner or in small groups. Pupils may need to
   share materials or may need the help of another pair of hands.

. Give pupils about 15 minutes to complete part 1. (Pupils who finish ahead
   of others can make designs with the shapes they cut out.)

. Discuss part 1 and compare answers. Teach the new word polyhedron by
   showing examples in the classroom. Some examples are filing cabinets, a
   closed crayon box, pyramids of Egypt, or ice cubes. Some non-examples are a
   cone, a baseball, a football, an egg, or a doughnut. If possible, have a
   rectangular block and a pyramid with a square base available to show pupils.
   (These polyhedrons are often included in commercial geometric solids sets.)

. Complete nos. 2 and 3 as a class. Have pupils complete the remaining problems on their own. Check paperwork by circulating among the pupils as they
   work or by sharing results as a class near the end of the math period.

Answers:

   1. (If 5 "shapes sheets" are used, the correct answers are given below.)

       25 squares
       25 small triangles
       15 tall triangles
       20 long rectangles

   2-5. See illustrations on pupil page for correct answer.

   6.   7. Answers will vary.